Clear the Clutter

Inge van der Ploeg

Clear the Clutter

Make Space for your Life

Floris Books

Translated from Dutch by Naomi Perlzweig

First published in 2004 by Floris Books
© 2004 Inge van der Ploeg

British Library CIP Data available

ISBN 086315-428-X

Printed in Great Britain
by Cromwell Press, Trowbridge

This book about household organization is the baton passed on to me by my mother and grandmother. I was instilled with their attitudes from living in their households. I have put these to practice and now offer the baton to those willing to take it.

Thanks so much to my Mother and Grandmother. Enjoy the book, dear readers.

Contents

Foreword

Come inside and make yourself at home

Just as I would greet a guest who enters my home, I offer the reader a warm welcome to my book, as you pass through its foreword. In *Clear the Clutter, Make Space for your Life,* you will encounter a wealth of ideas for organizing and maintaining a tidy household, as well as responses from my students and clients. You will also find exercises designed to help you explore the state of your own household. These are to help you and your housemates, or family members, become more aware of the objects in your home and how they are being treated.

Clients and students come to me continuously with questions on the subject. Some must adapt to decreased living space as a result of moving house. Others have less time than they had in the past, or, in some cases, even more time. Questions like these have inspired this book. The answers offered are based on my professional experience gained through my work at the Housekeeping Bureau, in Zeist, Holland.

The exercises are, I believe, unique, because they allow the reader to collaborate with the book. With this in mind, I recommend adding your own "tidying notebook" to the existing text, where you can record the exercises and jot down your own ideas and resolutions.

My thoughts with regard to tidying and household organization have been written to encourage new ideas in my readers, and have come to light in cellars, cupboards, during talks with clients, and during the musings that followed.

Once in a while, in the process of sifting and stacking at a client's home, the conversation takes a turn and the subject changes suddenly from flowerpots and old radios, and concealed stories start to surface and life's deeper purpose is revealed. This in turn provides insight and perspective. Such examples are described in the book.

You can keep notes in your tidying notebook and record your own story, but don't forget to write down your original ideas!

Cleaning up and making decisions whether to save or discard personal belongings requires some effort. It means deciding what you really want or need to make a well-considered choice. It's my sincere wish that this book will help you make choices that are both satisfying and liberating.

I am accustomed to introduce myself in the hallway when receiving a guest for the first time. So as you enter now, I will present myself to you.

I was born in the Netherlands in 1955, grew up in the town of Leeuwarden, and after leaving school attended the Sports Academy in Groningen, where I met my first husband, Johan. I taught physical education for eleven years, seven of which were in Leeuwaarden. Following Johan's death I moved to Zeist, and started afresh, working for the drug rehabilitation centre, Arta, as their Housekeeping Manager. The Housekeeping Bureau was founded, followed a year later by the establishment of the Efficiency Bureau. My research and experience in private homes — in the areas of tidying and household organization — is a service of the first bureau, which now offers courses on these subjects, in various locations throughout Holland. The "Personal Efficiency Program" for businesses is a service of the second bureau. This program is aimed at those who need help to organize office tasks and responsibilities effectively. For example, dealing with the mail (both conventional and email), establishing clear filing systems, organizing the computer in a systematic way, maintaining an over-view of tasks still to be done, planning an agenda and getting a grasp on work-related goals. There are efficiency trainers and "tidying co-workers" working with me in both companies.

I presently live in Amsterdam with Willem, whom I met while working on a tree-care project. As I've never had to run a busy household of my own, I've been able to channel my interest in the field of household organization into my professional life.

As you cross the threshold of the book you are naturally free to read it page by page, but you can also just skim through, read the tips and anecdotes, and do the exercises. The tone is both light and serious.

Enjoy your visit.

~ 1 ~

Hearth and Home

Where a genuine goddess
lends a helping hand

In ancient times, the site of the open fire was the central point of domestic life. This open fire, located precisely in the dwelling's centre was circular in form and could, therefore, be approached from all sides. This was the place for cooking, eating, conversing and singing together; visiting neighbours would sit around the fire. It was the children's play area, wet clothes would be hung to dry here and the local dog would keep watch.

In Amsterdam the first settlements, around 1180, consisted of small huts built from tree trunks and branches smeared with mud. The roofs were made of reeds or straw. The open fire was situated just over halfway into the dwelling: "The fire that one can go around". It was only when bricks were used as a building material and chimneys were built — after 1400 — that the hearth was placed at the side of the room, and the mantelpiece made its appearance. A draught partition built around the mantelpiece was the following step, which in the course of time developed into the so-called *binnen haert* "interior hearth", and so private quarters evolved within the home, which were more intimate than the communal entrance area. Consequently, the notion of "a home of your own" first developed; an old Dutch saying goes, "A hearth of your own is worth its weight in gold."

Time and attention, and obviously a fuel reserve, were key to tending to the fire. Wood was the most commonly used material for fuelling the fire, which involved sawing, chopping, splitting and stacking. The hearth was lit with a flint or a burning coal from another dwelling. Once a fire was burning a watchful eye was essential. It couldn't be allowed to blaze too fiercely and sparks had to be kept under control. To keep the fire going, it had to be fed regularly with new blocks of wood. Then there was the smoke, which had to be guided either upwards or outdoors. Sufficient heat was required for cooking on the fire, so the aim was to make optimal use of the fuel. Finally, the leftover ash was gathered and removed from the hearth. It was common practice in Saxon agriculture to allow the smouldering coals to burn until all the coal particles were reduced to ash. Properly burned ash served to enrich the soil, and was sifted and stirred for this purpose. The consistency of ash becomes almost like a liquid after stirring for approximately thirty minutes, at which point it could be spread over fields or gardens. In this way the vitality of the soil was sustained for centuries.

The responsibilities associated with tending to the hearth are functions of housekeeping. Housekeeping, however, does not end here. There's much more involved. Just think of tending to the needs of food, clothing and cleaning, and household administration is a modern addition. All this work calls for countless amounts of time and attention — day after day, week after week. And what's the impression left on other household members? Nobody even notices! When the household is running smoothly and the chores are done, we don't give it a second thought. Does anyone ever get commended for washing the dishes, cleaning the bathroom or making the beds? It's only when these matters aren't taken care of that awareness sets in … when there are no more clean glasses, or the clothes are all in the wash.

And so it goes. As soon as the problem has been dealt with and things are running smoothly, we take it all for granted again.

"Hope is not a requirement for endeavor, nor is success essential in order to persevere."

— William of Orange

Housekeeping is work that takes place behind the scenes. Anyone responsible for running a household — man or woman — knows this to be true. There's no end to it, it's repetitive, and no one ever bothers to say "thank you."

This out-of-sight and behind-the-scenes work was considered sacred three thousand years ago, embodied by the goddess, Hestia. Hestia resided on Mount Olympus and was the daughter of Kronos (Father Time) and Rhea (Mother of the Gods). Her brothers and sister were renowned for their heroic deeds: Zeus, followed his father as ruler of heaven and earth; Demeter, was guardian of the earth and its crops; and Poseidon was god of the sea. Fantastic sculptures have been made of these famous Greek gods, but not of Hestia. It is certain that she was worshipped by the common people in particular, but her image was hardly ever portrayed, although her being was self-evident as she represented hearth and home.

It has been said of Hestia that her work as caretaker gave her pleasure; she was never in a rush and took ample time to perform her activities and carried out all the household tasks, thus bringing peace and harmony into the home. Like the hearth itself, she was the energizing warmth accompanying the feeling of "home."

Since she had attained a state of self-fulfilment, with her gift of harmony giving her satisfaction, she needed no praise to motivate her.

This goddess has a peaceful, even meditative, experience

It's a pleasure to invite people over whether you live in your own house, apartment or under someone else's roof. It's a satisfying feeling to be able to present food, or offer a place to stay, to others. The house is charged with energy for days following an evening with a houseful of guests. Think of a house-warming party; having guests brings warmth to your home.

It's common practice to clean up before the guests' arrival. This is prompted by an expected visit. You want your guests to have ample space.

On the other hand, if you're not having much luck in keeping your house in order, this can affect hospitality. Some people are so ashamed of their mess that they'll only meet with others outside their home.

When visiting someone unexpectedly, you frequently hear, "Please ignore the mess." There are also those who keep the curtains and blinds closed in order to prevent others from seeing the condition inside.

The worst aspect of a house in disarray is the negative affect on hospitality. This is when Hestia-like skills can help you to bring order and space to your home, and they can be practised. Use the exercises given in this book for learning these skills, as they can help pave the way to becoming a good host or hostess.

In a well-known passage from Homer's *Odyssey*, Odysseus's son, Telemachus, goes in search of his father. After a long day's journey, he is welcomed at the castle of Menelaus. A wonderful description follows of the hospitality he receives, which was customary in those times. First his and his guides' horses are brought into the courtyard, and the guests are invited to bathe. Afterwards they're massaged with olive oil and given warm, dry clothes. Their hands are washed with warm scented water before being led to the host's table for a meal. They discuss events of the country and exchange news. Only after the meal's conclusion do the lord and lady of the castle ask Telemachus his name and ask after the purpose of his journey.

I'd like to compare this story to my standard reaction on opening the door when my doorbell rings. If it's a stranger, I expect him to explain the purpose of the call. My tone is matter of fact and if I'm in the right mood, I might crack a joke or exchange a few words with the individual. My patience is short-lived and I expect the person to make a quick exit, as I've got things to do. A cool reception, compared to the ancient Greeks, to say the least.

Hospitality is an expression of your home culture. Receiving guests — invited or uninvited — calls for hospitality. You offer free space, refuge and shelter. This is Hestia's domain.

to offer. If you're able to approach your work in this manner, your work will bring you in closer contact with yourself. And just as she did, you'll bring life's turmoil back to the central point — the hearth.

Hestia's fire burned in the home as well as the temple. This was her place, the central-point. The expression "fighting for hearth and home" has been in use for centuries. The centre of life is thus worth protecting.

During the era in which the Greek gods were worshiped, a fire was kept constantly burning in a public building. Fire could be taken from here to relight the home fires. When strangers came to town they visited this common hearth to become acquainted with their new surroundings and to warm themselves. Those who moved away took a coal with them to kindle a fire in their new community. There were also family rituals dedicated to Hestia.

A newborn child was carried around the hearth on the fifth day, followed by a meal of celebration. From that moment on the child was a fully-fledged member of the family and the town. Before a newly married couple could enter their new home, the mother of the bride preceded them with fire from her own hearth. The new pair moved in after the new hearth had been dedicated with this fire. Hestia's house was a home, a site of refuge, and a place of respite and peace.

It is evident that there is much more to living than those aspects symbolized by Hestia. We aspire to raise our children, study history or fight for a cause. We want to work and excel at something. Life is a mosaic of many parts, differing in colour and character and Hestia is one these. We honour that part by doing the daily, commonplace housekeeping. We honour her when the towels are clean and folded in the cupboard, the documents have been filed away, the boots are in the shed and when we are motivated to put our bank statements away in their folder and settle our business post, and last but not least, even when we empty the dishwasher while preparing breakfast.

It is evident when a household rests on a solid foundation, even in an unfamiliar house. You can sense when care is exercised. The impression of order is more than meets the eye. A mountain of chaos can be hidden behind an ordinary cupboard door, in a tidy room. Likewise a cluttered counter (that can be tidied in a flash) can camouflage a well-organized kitchen.

Even with piles of magazines strewn around the sofa it is possible that a backlog of tidying chores have all been taken care of. Hestia's silent, behind-the-scenes work is apparent in a house where someone is working calmly on the household rhythms.

I was the Housekeeping Manager for Arta — an organization in central Holland, offering voluntary rehabilitation to substance abusers. It was home to between fifteen and eighteen residents during the period I was employed there. My tasks included cleaning the big manor house and doing the washing and ironing together with five or six residents. We created a home-like atmosphere with artwork, both bought and home-made, flowers in vases and a Christmas tree in season.

It was also our job to clear the table after the coffee break. We would find it covered with sugar, spilled coffee, wastepaper and mud from outdoors. To try and reduce the mess I put a tablecloth on the table ... and it worked! With the tablecloth the table stayed clean much longer than without one. I was pleased with the outcome and considered ways to expand this principle —that is, to the principle of exercising care, which in turn leads to tidiness.

Together with my helpers, I then did a sort of investigation into three different rooms, carefully observing the dining room, hall and living room. Then, we stood with our eyes shut and just *listened*. Finally, we discussed where we felt care was lacking and any other thoughts that came up.

First of all, it was a surprise to discover that a room could be "listened to," and that a room could even communicate something. This obviously required a certain level of inner quiet and concentration (and some laughter control). Among other things we discovered that: the cupboard in the dining room was too dark; the sealed-off chimney was uninspiring; the living room hearth was too bare and there was too much commotion in the hallway.

During the discussion that followed, we decided on a strategy that we could tackle ourselves.

The hall was thoroughly cleaned and the residents hung paintings. We requested better lighting from the maintenance crew and asked them to remove the cupboard with cleaning supplies — though this proved a little more complicated. Christmas arrived shortly after and a colleague treated us to a flute performance. The changes made a real difference — the atmosphere was more conducive to conversation and appreciating someone else's creativity. All of these factors influence the mood in a house, and can be felt when you're there.

The above is a prime example of working on hearth and home in an effort to create harmony.

Hestia will re-appear throughout this book, as we need her fire and passion to undertake the tidying and other household chores. This book deals primarily with household organization, and the moment has now come to raise the flag under which this book sails.

✍ Exercise 1

The brick fireplace has replaced the hearth at the centre of a home. Central heating has even made the hearth obsolete, and does not keep a pot of coffee or tea hot, or provide a place to gather round with friends or family.

Ask yourself, where is the central point of your home?

Is the kitchen table the location where everyone collects to talk about their day? Does conversation and reading take place in front of the TV? Is the dining-room table the place where meals are eaten and games are played? Or maybe it's the table with the computer, or then again, an entirely different place in your home?

If you've picked out the spot — or maybe two — I'll ask you to devote extra attention and care to the place(s) you've pinpointed, for approximately four weeks, and carefully observe what goes on there during that period. Give the area a good clean. Don't go overboard, but take a calm approach, as Hestia would. Take a close look at aspects of cleanliness and breathing space by doing something about odours; put flowers there occasionally or add some extra colour. Contemplate the possibilities.

It helps to make a drawing, take a photo of the spot, or jot down your observations. It helps to take notes in a special notebook; it's easy to forget details in the space of four weeks time without a reminder. If you've kept at it, I recommend sharing your ideas with someone else after you've done this. This could be a housemate you're doing the exercise with, or just someone who happens to be interested. Don't discuss it during the process itself, but wait until the four weeks have passed. I've noticed that talking about it during the observation phase causes attention to slip away, while waiting, on the other hand, enhances your experience.

Juggling with Five Balls

The foundation of housekeeping

Housekeeping is a collective term, which covers too much to be summed up in one sentence. It includes everything needed to guarantee the smooth running of everyday living in the home. I visit many homes, usually at the request of the "woman of the house." If she has questions pertaining to household organization we walk through the house and examine all the jobs and problems we encounter on the way. If we make note of everything, the list can be lengthy. Where do you begin?

The Five Basics

I believe it's more important to find the right rhythm for doing the ironing and dishwashing than to deal with the eight boxes of unknown contents in the attic. I also give priority to this year's photographs over ones taken fourteen years ago.

The backlog of odd jobs must be taken care of, but it shouldn't cause you to fall even farther behind. This means that you should keep up with the daily and weekly work; you need rhythm to keep it in motion. Settling bills, doing the laundry, cleaning the bathroom and maintaining the central heating come first.

How to tackle the less urgent tasks with which you have fallen behind is discussed in Chapter Seven.

This chapter is called "Juggling with Five Balls." In my elementary school days, ball games were popular. Later I learned to juggle with three balls. Occasionally I see a street acrobat juggling five balls or even with fire. Fantastic! This is an inspiration for housekeeping when you consider that here too, there are five "balls" to keep airborne: Food, clothing, maintenance, cleaning and the post. These are the five pillars for everyday living.

When you're in charge of a household you are the manager and these five aspects are vital to the business. You might attend to them yourself, with your housemates or family members, or hire an outside service. At some point you might need an advisor. In times past this was the woman next-door offering advice from over the garden fence. This book serves the same purpose. Whatever fits your situation, you are the key figure, unless of course you share the job with your partner. In that case there are two managers, each with individual responsibilities. Regular consultation helps to give you both a view of the total picture. When the duties regarding these five aspects are running smoothly and there's no backlog, you have reason to be satisfied. You are taking care of the foundation of living. But how do you keep your daily business running smoothly? Let's move on.

✔ TIP

A student has a shopping list on her computer containing items that she buys frequently. The list corresponds with the layout of the store where she does most of her shopping. She prints out this list and checks off what she needs before going shopping. This, of course, can also be done without a computer. All you have to do is make a copy of your list.

Food

People need all sorts of nourishment. We consume food and drink to sustain our bodies; we listen to the music we love and to blackbirds singing in the evening.

✓ TIP

Establishing holiday rituals brings families together and creates a source of future pleasant memories. Here are two examples.

One of my clients has her grandmother's exquisite Christmas crockery. Every November, she takes it out of its box, which is kept at the bottom of a cupboard in a storage room. At the end of January it is replaced again. This unpacking and repacking has become a festive winter ritual.

Another winter ritual: There's a Christmas dinner tradition in Laurence's family. In a corner of the kitchen at the end of November there appear countless ingredients and recipes to bake the most delicious Christmas cookies. When her children were old enough, they wanted to bake cookies too. This has been going on for some years now, and when someone happens to have clean hands and a little time, the weighing, mixing and baking can begin.

Our eyes welcome an appetizing sight, we satisfy our sense of smell and taste and breathe fresh air into our lungs. In short, we nourish ourselves. Everything enters us via our mouth and our senses. This brings us to the subject of food.

Before a meal we do the shopping or pick fruit and vegetables from the garden. We bring these to the kitchen to prepare the meal, and store foods in the pantry, cupboard or freezer.

After eating we wash the dishes, and the pots and pans. We take the refuse to the trash or compost, put the recyclables away and save empty bags in a drawer. In order to accomplish this we need space and objects, whose purpose is to serve us. Do you have a handy shopping list in the kitchen? Does cold storage for vegetables exist, and are there many items in the kitchen unrelated to food preparation? Are breakfast ingredients easy to reach, so that the children can reach them without needing help when setting the breakfast table? Examine all the segments of your food connection. Ask yourself if there's enough space and appropriate tools at hand. The rest of the objects you encounter can most likely be put away somewhere else. Make your daily work environment a comfortable one.

Being practical and staying on top of things can be a sport. Consider the following examples:

One of my neighbours has a blackboard in her bathroom for writing her shopping list — maybe this is the principle of first discarding before acquiring something new; one girlfriend plans all the meals for the week on Sunday and then goes shopping for the whole week on Tuesdays and Fridays. I also know people who participate in a vegetable box system where they have no control over the assortment of vegetables, thus avoiding the predicament of having to decide on a menu in advance.

My friend, Agnes, however, wins hands down. She is a gardener, and her household, though sober, generates a different kind of wealth. Her kitchen cupboards are practically empty, and contain three serving dishes, some stacked bowls and four pans, with is more than enough space in-between. An impression of simplicity arises because there's never too much, and a feeling of wealth stems from her generosity. We eat at her home sometimes. She makes her appearance with stew, warm bread, homemade herb butter and apple pastry from the oven. The table is decorated with brass candlesticks holding red candles, and flowering branches in a vase. You feel the abundance of nature around you. It's a genuine pleasure, and her cupboards are spaciously arranged.

Washing the dishes

During a course the subject turned to jobs like dish-washing. Which rhythm works best to keep dirty dishes under control? We concluded that this calls unavoidably for a daily rhythm.

If you wait any longer it takes more time in the long run, when you consider the scraping and scrubbing, not to mention running out of forks and glasses. One of my students decided to empty the dishwasher when preparing breakfast. She switches it on in the evening to wash the day's dishes, and in the morning she empties it and starts the new day. This rhythm was so agreeable that it only took a small effort to keep with it, until it became a matter of course. The point is to discover a workable rhythm for your tasks — with or without a dishwasher.

Clothing

The subject of clothing is a similar story. This too is a daily and weekly job with its own hurdles to overcome. You buy clothes or make them yourself, wear them, throw them in the laundry and wash and dry them. Then there's the folding, ironing, mending and putting away.

The first problem comes up if you buy or acquire too

✔ TIP

A schoolteacher I know claims he has breakfast prepared in two minutes. Making the breakfast and doing the shopping on Saturdays are his household responsibilities. His family has seven members. He's discovered the following system for organizing breakfast during the morning rush: He does most of the preparation the evening before — he sets the table, makes the children's lunch boxes, and fills the kettle. In the morning he gets dressed, puts the water on to boil and puts part of the breakfast ingredients on the table. He goes back upstairs to shave, then gets the remainder of breakfast out of the fridge and pours the coffee and tea. It's a good start to the day, with an accomplished mission, every single morning. The children take their own dirty dishes to the kitchen counter.

much. Where are you supposed to store it all? Not to mention the unique pieces of material, bought at bargain prices.

When it comes to clothing and its care, however, we usually get stuck in the ironing and mending department. That's
where to find the hold-up.

A client told me that she and her husband bought an
incredible amount of shirts and underwear because there
were never any in the cupboard. When her son, daughter-in-
law and grandchild came to stay over, she cleaned out the
laundry, which also served as a guest room — and I bet
you've guessed the rest. All the forgotten pieces re-appeared,
some with loose seams, others with stains requiring treat-
ment, others with missing buttons or in need of ironing, etc.

Do you have three hampers — one for the whites, one for
coloured clothes and one for hand-washing? Are they near to
where people dress and undress so that piles don't accumulate along the way? Is there a policy about using the hampers
so that your partner and children co-operate? When is the
laundry done? At night, when rates are off-peak, or only on
Saturdays? One student realized that she did the washing the
moment someone complained that his or her vital pair of
jeans was in the laundry. Consequently, she was washing
seven to eight times a week. So, she decided to employ a
steady rhythm, which meant doing a full load every evening
that was hung up to dry before breakfast the next morning.
This is how she kept up with the laundry to her and her family's satisfaction.

I want to add an example regarding my husband and the ironing. He has wonderful memories of the smell of freshly ironed
laundry, which is definitely connected with his mother and
aunts and pleasant childhood associations. One evening I was
standing ironing — I work sitting down nowadays, as advised
by an old home economics teacher — while he was home. Just
for fun, he took out his flute and played some Handel for me.

✓ Tip

Going through a summer wardrobe each October can be an enjoyable ritual. If you're not going to wear certain items again until the following April, you can store them in a box or bag. Your cupboard will then only contain clothes for the next six months.

Come April, you can go through the winter items and take out what you won't be wearing during the summer season. Air them for a day and store them in their designated place, taking measures to protect against moths, humidity and rodents. Your wardrobe will then be more spacious.

It's a nice surprise to rediscover the contents of your summer clothing box after winter storage; airing, assessing, mending, giving away, searching for a matching shirt or saving something for your youngest child, are all aspects of a twice-yearly clothing project. If you're doing this for others as well as yourself, label the bags to facilitate easy re-location if something is needed in-between.

It was a special treat that I still think back on with pleasure. This just illustrates how we can make routine jobs more appealing for each other. To avoid any misunderstandings, he also helps with the ironing.

Do you do all the ironing yourself? How many times a week, and do you work sitting? Thinking of my old teacher made me appreciate a neighbour's suggestion. She has a small room with a TV and an ironing board with a chair in front of it. This just fits in that room. She's combined the tip about working sitting down with watching a favourite programme.

A client with four adolescents at home distributes the clean wash in her children's rooms according to owner. An ironing board is set up in the upstairs hall, which can be used as needed. A quick ironing lesson can make a big difference in the long run.

I sometimes take my mending to my parent's or a girl-friend's house. I bring along my sewing basket along with one or two items, which I've been putting off. This works for me. I can either just talk and have fun or talk while doing something useful and still have fun.

The mending never stops piling up. A client offered the best tip I've ever heard on the subject.

She has a sewing kit hanging from her ironing board. Each loose button or seam gets repaired at once. The message is: do it while it's still minor and try to make the conditions favourable with friends or music.

Cleaning

Cleaning is the third standard job at home. It has a routine character. How many times have you ever washed the floors, cleaned the bathroom or washed yourself? There's a wealth of tips in all sorts of books, including titles with advice from our grandmothers' time. There are special cleaning materials and cleansing agents — some more or less aggressive than others — on the market. These are made for hygiene, spot and stain removal, giving fresh odours and parasite prevention.

Cleaning can be characterized by habit and routine. Some tasks are most conveniently performed on certain days of the week; for example, the bedrooms on Saturday, and the bathroom on Tuesday. If you have cats or dogs and your daughter happens to be asthmatic, if you live in a sandy area or your entrance opens directly on to the garden, it may be necessary to sweep and vacuum more often than if you live in an upstairs apartment.

I'm reminded of a client who told me that she started a daily housekeeping hour with her husband and five children. Every-day after supper everyone is given a task from a list in the kitchen. This list is rotated every two months. There's something for everyone: folding the laundry, sweeping and straightening the hall, cleaning the bathroom, clearing the table, washing the dishes and vacuuming the living room. Everyone, large and small participate, even friends and overnight guests. A bell is rung to mark the hour's end, and then it's time for a refreshment break. The table-talk resumes and then everyone goes their own way — to do homework, put children to bed, to read the paper, to play outside or to choir practice. This is how one mother keeps the daily chores in motion. She has a positive outlook, which encourages good work attitudes among her family. As long you stick to a rhythm for the chores, you won't get behind. I read the following in a housekeeping magazine: "The best way to keep house is to keep up with the housekeeping."

Maintenance

House maintenance includes small do-it-yourself jobs or larger ones, often contracted out. It all depends on your skills, time and budget.

Fittings, light bulbs and batteries should be on hand. Do you have a permanent place to store these items, or are you someone who always wonders if the battery on the counter is new or used? Is there a place for tools and do they get put away after use? Do you take proper care of your paint and brushes so that they can be re-used?

My friend Liz is terrific at organizing a "chore day" on Saturdays. She invites over handy friends, appoints her brother to be in charge of tools and caters the event herself. Everyone fixes and paints while having a good time, as working on odd jobs together can bolster friendship.

If you want to determine which job has priority, just ask yourself which unfinished chore has been bothering you most. If there's a loose plank that you seem to be constantly tripping over then place that at the top of your list. Following a logical sequence is essential. Paint the ceiling before you lay the carpet and after the room has been emptied. Do-it-yourself books and brochures from specialist shops also contain practical advice.

You can arrive at your plan with the help of lists. Write down the chosen strategy and hang it on the kitchen door. Then it's time to get on with it — confer with housemates or family members, make preparations, organize, go over estimates and do the jobs you're able to yourself. The plan might need adjustment, items may get crossed off the list and new problems could arise.

Maintenance actually means "supporting or protecting." A draught is undesirable, and who needs a leaking pipe or faucet? What we do want is reliable plumbing, a sound electrical system and, naturally, a source of heat. The list is endless and there's so much to be had in the western world. Attend to details with the help of your to-do list. Finishing a chore is an activity that brings well-being to you and your home. Completing a project renews energy. It does however require an effort to strip wallpaper, fill holes in the walls, scrape the loose paint off the woodwork, apply a new coat of paint, clean the paint brushes and put them away.

When a journalist asked a top government figure for the source of his endless energy he thoughtfully replied: "I attribute my energy to the fact that I finish what I start." The project you take on has to be carefully assessed. Can you foresee what you're getting into? This man's "antenna" was geared to anticipating this factor. He obviously also knew how to persevere. This can be learned. Experience teaches you to estimate how much time is needed to finish a new job by looking back at a previous one. How long did it actually take to paint the room? This knowledge can help you to make a realistic estimation before taking on the following job. You might also just chance it: "Oh, painting that room, that's about a weekend's work." Multiply the estimated time by three!

✍ **Exercise 2**

Walk through your house with a pen and notepad. Take a good look at each space and write down what you want changed. When you return to your starting point write down each chore on a separate piece of paper; old calling cards are also handy. Lay them on the table as you would in a card game and arrange them according to your answers to the following questions:

What can I do myself?
When can I do it? (use your appointment diary)
What are the preparations that have to be made?
What can I ask others — friends, family and housemates to do?
What needs to be contracted out; who is the contractor; what are the costs involved?

My own lists, by the way, took four Saturdays to complete and one week to sink in. Your instinct for it improves by making a point of reviewing previous experience. If you find that you're missing your target too often, you can use a household notebook. Make sure it has a fixed place in the house. Just for fun and to practice using your "antenna" note the amount of time you've estimated for a particular job, as that's how this story began.

Mail

The fifth and last of the basics is the mail. The mailbox, email and fax all bring various messages into your home. Has anyone ever tried to figure out how much this amount of paper weighs every week? They start off in a pile, on top of the hall cupboard, or on a corner of the piano, and include business and personal mail.

This morning I received: a thank-you note from my godchild

TIP

If you want to go through the mail or do administrative chores, sit down first.

for a wedding gift; a bank statement; a confirmation for a convention; and an invoice for my disability insurance.

This pile contains administrative work that needs to be done. I save business chores for Friday evenings. There's a shelf under my desk where I put the things that have to be dealt with, but can wait till Friday. This is when I get as much as I can out of the way. I put the finished work away in its folder. The following Friday I deal with the rest. I use a system of hanging folders, and have a special drawer for bank statements. A letter from a girlfriend in Africa doesn't land on this shelf. I read it and write back to Irene during a free moment, because I enjoy doing it. I also have a shelf for outgoing mail. This includes envelopes with bank checks, things to take to the office and things to put away in the house.

One of my clients is horrified by her mail. She felt threatened by it, and stopped emptying the mailbox and opening the mail. She just couldn't get herself to deal with it. And who could blame her? The closing date has been and gone and she still hasn't submitted her income tax return. Every Tax Authority envelope that lands on her doormat seemed to be sneering at her. She opens it and finds it's only the reminder for her car tax. What a relief!

What we receive in the post can be overwhelming. Some people put notices on their front doors demanding that unsolicited mail should not be delivered. It's like a wild animal in need of taming. Ask a friend or a colleague how they deal with their mail. Let's leave it at that for now. I'll continue with this topic later in the book.

I have now been through the five basics, which keep a household moving along. Any backlogs within these processes should be dealt with first.

In the food section, I've illustrated how to follow a similar course of action from start to finish. Is there enough space and appropriate material to optimally perform the necessary actions?

You can examine all five basics to see if this is the case. In other words, organize things so that they work for you. That way your routines will run more smoothly and you'll be able to perform them as a matter of course. What are the consequences if your container for recyclable paper is a long way from where you open your mail? Piles develop in-between, which won't improve anybody's mood.

As a manager you should make use of your skills to juggle these five balls, like a performing artist. Sometimes you have to gently hit the proper ball. With adequate organization the balls keep falling rhythmically as you continue to juggle, but there's more to a circus than the juggling act. The lions are coming home from school and the acrobat from work. Your outside job may demand trapeze-like skills, but your job at home seems to never reach its conclusion. Just like life, housework goes on.

Cleaning a room improves hygienic conditions and influences your perception of space, as you have perhaps observed. When you clean up the corner of a room — cleaning, tidying and rearranging — the room appears more spacious, making you feel more comfortable than before. It can be an inspiration to create something new, which I discovered with children I had in my care after thoroughly clearing out, cleaning and reorganizing their play corner. That day, after coming home from school, they began to play with fresh interest and concentration. The newly-tidied corner had a real and positive affect.

When I was about twenty-five, parents and teachers at the school where I taught gave the classrooms a thorough clean in the week before the summer vacation. We painted, scrubbed and did repairs. The school shone so brightly that it almost made you squint. We were a very satisfied group following that week of work and exertion, and for a brief moment we thought we could keep it in the same condition. The children would be back the following Monday and after all, that's why we had gone to all that trouble! It was that pleasant kind of anticipation. The floor was clean and bright and had even been freshly waxed, and then the feet with shoes marched in. But that's the way it's supposed to be. You perform an act of caring and then you let go; it's like breathing in and then out. Cleaning is to benefit people, not just for the sake of cleanliness.

What I actually did was to clean away a certain element of its past and make way for its future. There's a transitional area between these two points, which you reach by scrubbing, washing, tidying, fixing and completing a task. In this way you help to prepare your world at home for the future. Even though the people you live with may not notice, life itself knows what you're doing, because life is good, thanks to you.

Routines

Routines are a major aid to housekeeping chores, and keep all the non-stop work in motion. If you don't have routines you can learn them. As you read the different tips and advice in this book, I can just imagine you thinking: "Okay, sounds good, but try sticking with it!" There are always things that come up and frustrate the best-laid plans, and moreover ... routines are boring.

Nonetheless, I want to make a case for routines. You

undoubtedly have more than ten in your own household, you are just unaware of them. A routine is simply too ordinary, and that's precisely its advantage. You don't have to think twice about where to find your toothbrush; it's on the bathroom sink. You take a spoon from the cutlery drawer, and put it back after it's been washed. These things are so commonplace, your hands know what to do; there is no need to bother your mind.

After moving house, you literally experience the habits that your arms and legs have already acquired. You feel somewhat lost in a new house at first. You walk upstairs to get the vacuum cleaner before you realize that it's kept downstairs in the new house. Even after reorganizing in a familiar house, you will notice that old habits seem to linger before you get accustomed to the changes.

Do you have any idea how long it takes before a new habit is acquired? Do you ever make an attempt to change your handwriting? Imagine that you want to change the way you write your "g" or your "r." What about brushing your teeth with your left hand, instead of your right? Try it some time. How much time is needed before a new habit becomes routine? Rhythms are intuitive in humans. Just think about wak-

 TIP

While implementing the habit towards which you've chosen to work, you might discover that you've made the wrong choice.

Be happy with this discovery. Give yourself a moment to reflect. After all, the point is to improve your situation. You can always decide later to make changes regarding the habit in question (or break it completely). Whatever helps you to reach your goals is okay. Practicing is a way of making things better, not more difficult.

ing up at daylight and feeling sleepy when it gets dark. A woman's reproductive cycle is also rhythmical. Feeling a slump at four-thirty in the afternoon is a rhythm, and as I once read in a humorous book, so is getting drunk at four! People are constantly faced with recurring rhythms, which influence their lives.

It's a similar story with habits. The number forty has a special significance for people. It takes approximately six weeks, or forty days, for a new resolution to be integrated into our systems. However with perseverance it will settle and stick. It's an incubation period of sorts, but for habits.

Imagine you're fed up confronting the dirty dishes in the dishwasher every morning. You could fill it in the evening, turn it on at night and empty it in the morning, while you're getting breakfast ready. You decide to do it this way every day. It then takes six weeks to "teach your hands." Make a note in your diary or appointment calendar for six weeks. Remind yourself of your resolution. Share it with your housemates or ask for their support. Working with others is effective and good for motivation. What's important is to stick to your resolution for forty days. If you lapse during this period, correct yourself as soon as you realize what's happened, and start again. It has to become part of your system. Sometimes it only takes four weeks and sometimes you'll need six. You'll find out. If you feel that something is missing when the dishwasher hasn't been emptied, then you've come a long way towards acquiring the new habit. Maintaining a habit gets easier with time. If you stop doing it for a while, it will slip away again. Your actions are like a plant, which needs repeated, routine watering.

During a recent visit, I saw various photos, postcards, a poem, two reproductions and hand-written messages on the bathroom's tiled walls. One of these contained the following words: "Discipline is allowing habits to be born continu-

✍ Exercise 3

Make a resolution regarding a new habit you want to cultivate. For instance, setting the breakfast table the evening before or making a key rack for keys that you use regularly. Write down your decision in your appointment diary on that very date, and start the chore. Write your objective in your diary six weeks further on. Don't forget to make a note on the pages of the final week; start to make plans for your "celebration" if that's an incentive. Tell someone else about your plan and the date your exercise period ends. He or she could also make note of that date in his or her diary. Do you need more support? What works best for you? Maybe it's having someone send you a card or calling you halfway through to give you encouragement. Make the necessary arrangements.

Now the forty-day period begins: If you have a diary you can follow your own actions on paper. This is a helpful tool for looking back later on. Write down the habit you aspire to acquire and the date at the end of this chapter on a post-it note. This will be fun to read when you come across it again in the future.

ously." The woman who lived there had completed a course in household organization!

I came across a good tip in Yolanda Eigenstein's book, *The Happy Worker*. In her business, it's customary to celebrate a successful assignment. If you set a goal for yourself — for instance, updating your appointment diary every Sunday evening — and it seems to have become a habit after six weeks, then it's time for a treat. You can celebrate alone or with others. Just make sure you take the time to enjoy your successful efforts. A student of mine treated herself to flowers after tidying three cupboard shelves. Neither the clean-up nor the flowers were commonplace occurrences, and she was delighted with both.

It's healthy to mark the full-stops and commas in your life. It turns the ordinary into something interesting and pleasant. Why shouldn't you? It's a celebration to buy yourself flowers or to get comfortable on the sofa with a book and a cup of tea, or whatever else is special for you.

Routines are especially helpful in tackling recurrent jobs such as folding laundry, watering plants and feeding the cat. All those chores you can qualify as "over and over" work most effectively by applying rhythms, which can be practiced until they become habits.

Rhythm is alternating "doing" and "not doing." After consuming food a period of digestion follows, then comes a rest phase before you feel hungry again. It's the same principle when you clean the staircase and then forget about it for a while. The stairs are walked on and dust forms once more. Then you notice the dust and feel inclined to clean again. How much time does it take before the dust starts swirling in your house? Is it a week, less than a week or more? Dealing with the washing, your plants, the staircase and the empty bottles is like the swing of a pendulum; caring for, using, cleaning and then letting it go again. It's a never-ending process. Just like breathing, it goes on and on. It's either activity or inactivity.

You wear shoes to walk outdoors. You take them

> ✓ TIP
>
> One of my students changed her buying behaviour following her home clean-up. Before buying, she now considers how long the object in question is expected to last, and then asks herself if she's willing to take on responsibility for that length of time.

off at home and let them air. This helps to keep them in good condition. You take your clean, dry sheets from the line or dryer, fold them and put them in the linen cupboard. "Sheets need a rest too," a client was once told by her grandmother. So they go in and out of the cupboard and the pause in-between gives breathing space to life. If the basic household tasks are done rhythmically it can feel liberating.

Things change during the course of your life; your children grow older; you acquire new hobbies and through this the habits, which help you to juggle five balls, also undergo change.

During my job at the drug rehabilitation centre vacation plans were made for the residents and staff. While getting ready for the trip a discussion about personal habits came up among the women. We spoke of how we did things as individuals, i.e. dressing and undressing, how often we showered, etc. I remember that conversation as one of the finest ones during the time I worked there. Even though the topic seemed so commonplace it wasn't for us. Hearing about each other's habits gave us the mutual trust needed for our trip together. We learned that: one of us would not be seen in public without make-up; that I preferred washing in the evenings; that someone wanted to brush her teeth after every meal; and another liked to walk outdoors every morning in her pyjamas to check the weather.

These are matters we don't normally discuss, just because habits are so habitual. If you do, however, you suddenly gain more insight into your own behaviour. Consequently, you have more of a tendency to accept others. I would recommend doing the same if you go on vacation with people you don't usually share a roof with. We didn't get on each other's nerves, at least not with regard to the topics shared during that talk.

I once observed Lent — the days between Ash Wednesday and Easter — with a group of people by participating in a fast. However, we did it a little differently than is customary among Catholics. We wrote down what we wanted to clean up within ourselves and thought of an appropriate exercise. We then folded up the pieces of paper and put them in a closed container.

On Easter Saturday, a good six weeks later, the container was opened. We sat in a circle with the container in the middle; everyone unfolded their paper and read what they'd written. The stories about striving, forgetting and changing were read out loud — I want to refrain from buying books for myself for six weeks; I want to look at myself in the mirror every morning and tell myself I'm worthwhile; I want to notice and appreciate the trees and streams every day. There were scores of examples. Everyone had kept his or her own goal to themselves in the period in-between. What we heard was very revealing about each person.

Described here is a cleansing of sorts; it's purifying and revitalizing, but for your inner self. I remembered that we had given ourselves a day off from our assignment on Easter Sunday, but no one thought it necessary.

If the basic rhythms are in motion, how do you go about tackling the backlog of work?

How do you actually go about cleaning up? What do you save and what should you discard?

Let's take out a magnifying glass and take a closer look at our things.

Migrating objects

The road things travel, in your home and in your life

Objects flow through your house like a river. You lead a busy life and thus create a trail of used things, and then you pick them up again. Refuse from the garden goes on the compost heap and used paper napkins are thrown in the trash. How do things migrate from one place to another without legs? We keep moving them from place to place. There's always something in our hands, on the verge of being put somewhere.

If you could attach a camera to an object, for example, to an umbrella, and then follow the route it takes, you would see the story of its "life." Using our imagination that's just what we're going to do, while we follow the course a head of lettuce or our aunt's old teapot might take. Don't believe for a moment that objects are inert; they move about under your roof, and it's interesting to observe the course they take. You'll soon discover the areas in which your household is functioning properly and where the back-ups and jams occur. Things get tossed around, pile up, disappear from view or get lost. They're always doing something. How does this happen? The process can be compared to how our bodies process food.

A student's young son was playing with a friend and was intensely absorbed in their games. The floor was scattered with toys and it was almost 5.30 pm, the time the friend had to go home.

"Are you guys going to clean up now?" the woman asked the boys.

"Don't pay attention to my Mom," the son told his friend. "She's taking a course."

At a certain point things enter your house. You may buy vegetables, pick strawberries from your garden or a friend might give you flowers that you want to put in the kitchen. You put the flowers in a vase you once received as a gift from your grandmother. Think of the messages that enter your house by conventional post via the mailbox or email via the computer. One way or another it all makes its way inside. You buy, receive, inherit, borrow or find things and then bring them home. Things enter through the "skin" of your household.

✔ TIPS

Create a permanent spot for incoming mail — if necessary make sure each household member has one for her or himself. Open shelves with individual (letter size) compartments are handy.

Shop with a list

Are you cautious about what you acquire? Do you buy too quickly or accept too easily?

Are you a beachcomber or do you borrow a lot owing to your many interests? How many papers or magazines do you subscribe to?

Do you have the nerve to say, "No?"

A family with two children lived on welfare for years. They had always welcomed everything that they were given. Among the articles received were toys, an old camera, magazines and various items that others didn't want anymore. The mother, whom I'll call Angela, was happy to take what she got.

When she found a paying job, the family's spending power gradually increased and a marked improvement took place. Saving for a bicycle and taking care of shoe repairs were now both feasible. They could even take a real vacation. Their frugal life was on the way out, but an open attitude remained. Angela still accepted everything that she was given. Her friends and acquaintances were accustomed to automatically give bags of "useful" goods to Angela. These acts of acceptance ultimately reached enormous proportions. The house was slowly experiencing an overload and space was getting scarce. Looking for a clean t-shirt in a cupboard was like groping through chaos. For the first time questions arose: What do we keep and what has to go? Am I prepared to sort through everything or is it too much? What should we do with all this useful stuff? This was the start of a search for new balance, between in and out, yes and no.

Consumption

To compare the process of "entering" with the process that food undergoes in our bodies, we can use the physiological term, "to consume." When eating you take a bite of food. If it's too spicy, prickly or bad tasting, you spit it out immediately. This is an automatic and natural reaction, which protects your body, for example, from sharp fish bones that can damage tissue. It also protects you from substances that are poisonous, indigestible and harmful. It's just as natural to return unwelcome items at the front door. However, "spitting out" in this case is not quite as automatic. Before you know it, you've got a

TIP

Stop putting things away temporarily and put them in their proper place today

bag full of climbing boots for your three boys, which you've received from a well-meaning neighbour, even though they already have perfectly good climbing boots.

If you're the recipient of too many things, your home becomes saturated. A log jam can develop in your hallway and the floor gets flooded with things. Does your hallway contain piles of post and bags of items to be sorted out, in addition to coats and shoes, or even a shopping bag? If so, they're in your way. What can you do about it? What should you swallow and what would you rather spit out?

Warming-up

If food is accepted by your mouth, you chew and swallow it. Once inside it reaches body temperature, is digested, and things like orange pips are discarded. Similarly, you

TIP

Are you a beachcomber? Do you bring home the most fantastic items you've found on the street or at the beach? It's not unusual that an old chair only warms up after it's been sanded and painted red. Found objects have the tendency to collect dust. Renewal helps to prevent this.

can decide which things to keep. Unwanted items can go directly to the recycle bin if appropriate, the back door or the garage, to be dealt with later. I call the process of accepting new objects "warming-up." You take the shopping from your bags, put the vegetables in the refrigerator, bread in the bread-bin and light bulbs in the cupboard. You give everything a place. In other words, *warmth* is making sure that the "temperature" of everything is right and that objects entering your house are hospitably welcomed. Maybe you recognize this idea at the check-in desk at the airport. The baggage is placed on a conveyor belt, is labelled, and then moves on to its destination. Are your methods comparable, or does the post stay stuck in a pile?

I know a child who received a sweater from her grandmother for her birthday. She unwrapped it and looked at it with pleasure, obviously happy with her gift. She then proceeded to wrap it up again and left it in her room for days. She put it on for the first time two weeks later. She needed time to really get familiar with it, to truly make it hers. There are also children, as well as adults, whose warming-up process is much quicker. In the case of the sweater they would put it on immediately, or even want to wear it to bed. The difference in individuals is fun to observe. In my own case, I recognize both, the slow and the fast warm-up.

> ✔ TIP
>
> An empty worktop is a feasible goal if all the loose objects cluttering it get their own specific place. It's the same story with a desktop, if all the papers in the drawers or in the cupboard have their own place in a file or hanging folder.

I also have personal experience with a "bad buy." A bad buy is something you've bought that won't warm-up no matter what you try. It just doesn't feel right, even after doing your best to make it work. On a certain level you're saying "no" to it, and in this case it's advisable to find it a different home. All the things in your house that you don't really want can cause a log-jam if you don't act. I'll get back to this in the following chapter.

Digestion

We speak of digestion as the process that follows the swallowing of food. Food passes through the stomach and intestines, changes consistency and is broken down. The digestive organs work virtually unnoticed during this process. In our home, this "digestion," or more accurately, using and wearing (out), also take place unnoticed. We wear our shoes and they wear out. We even read certain books until they fall apart. We only take notice when something is actually broken or torn. We then repair it or have it repaired. My mother received a silver fork as a gift for her eighteenth birthday, and she's used it nearly every day since. Tiny shavings invisible to the eye have worn off from sixty years of use. My father's intensive use of his spoon has had a similar effect. His spoon is now so thin that it can be bent effortlessly.

A fork can last a lifetime, a painting for generations and a city bicycle only a year or two. An apple or a head of lettuce won't make it quite that long. They'll be eaten sometime during the week. Everything that exists has its own lifetime and wearing-out time. Things at home are directly connected to life at home during the "digestive" stage, and fulfil a supporting role. That's why we bring them home in the first place! When clothes in need of mending remain too long in the mending basket and are out of circulation, a jam or back-up can develop.

Making Choices

If something is worn or broken, it might be repairable. Shoes can be re-soled and a windowpane can be replaced. However, at a certain point, the question arises: "Is it worth saving?"

Our intestines ask the same question. Should this substance be eliminated from, or kept within, the body? Keeping or discarding is a choice. This elimination process occurs in the middle of the seven processes described in this chapter. It's just as crucial to the feeling of well-being in your home as it is to your body. Deciding to keep or discard household objects leads to the question: "Do I want to keep this or would I rather have the space it takes up?"

If you entered the work-shed of my childhood home,

> ✔ **TIP**
>
> Sorting through a box of items to choose what to keep or not goes quicker when you tackle the job with another person.
>
> Do you feel you have too much and that possessing costs you too much energy? Read *Simplify Your Life*, Elaine St. James.

you'd see a row of old baby-food jars screwed to the bottom of a shelf by their lids. My sister and I ate the original contents and my father saved the jars for storing thick screws, long screws, crosshead screws, wire nails and upholstery tacks. There were hundreds of them, and they stayed put until they were needed.

People with large homes tend to save casually because their living space is sufficient. If your living quarters are small or limited because of the number of people living there, the problem is more pressing. Even the most efficient of systems can encounter an overload. What do you do then? The term "storage system" is a hard one to define. Anyone can store things. You put them somewhere and that's it. However, finding them again four years later is a different story. Is your storage system

---

It's customary in Slovenia to tell people, who are about to throw something away: "Think first, you'll need it again in seven years."

> **✓ TIP**
>
> My parents, sister and I used to camp out on an island. In the beginning we took a tent but had a trailer later on. My mother would pack and assign us each our own colour. My toothbrush, cup, dish and towel were red; my sister's were blue, my mother's yellow, and my father's green. It was a practical system, which we took for granted.

an effective finding-back-again system? Do you store something away knowing that you'll have forgotten about it four years from now?

Chapter Five deals exclusively with the subject of making choices to save or discard. If making choices is easy for you, the one concerning "keeping or getting rid of" is quickly determined. If you're someone who struggles with indecision, here are some considerations that can help you to make the right choices. Questions on this subject are normal. Life changes bring new changes as to whether to save or discard. Questions from an earlier period are then resolved.

Saving

We speak of keeping or saving when a choice is made to preserve or store something. You can make jam from a surplus of strawberries from your garden. The pots are then stored in a storage cupboard or pantry. I store Christmas decorations until Christmas rolls around again, and my tent until I get the urge to go camping. I also save my skating prizes from years gone by, but for nostalgia's sake.

First food was canned and later frozen. Both methods were for preserving food for future use. We save to benefit us in times to come. Our bodies store as well. If you eat more than you need, fatty tissue builds up as an energy reserve, which can be converted into sugar in times of need. This gives our cell metabolism the energy and warmth needed by our bodies, and is a normal physiological reaction. If you feel like you're storing too much in your home and your attic looks like a warehouse, you may have to take a step back and

> ### ✔ TIP
>
> One student picks up all his miscellaneous newspapers and magazines every Thursday to deposit them in the recycle bin. If someone wants to save something or cut out an article, they're advised to do it before Thursday.

make choices. Saving is an art in itself. It calls for resources and awareness. This will be dealt with in Chapter Six.

Growth and Development

You cut out an article because you consider it to be useful or meaningful. You can make something from a certain piece of material you've saved, and when you find it again you can apply your sewing skills and creativity. You save a pot of jam for a special sweet sauce to accompany Christmas dinner. You made the jam in the summer and it keeps well. During certain parts of the year — or your life — you create conditions for another. Thoughtful care along these lines serves life well, making richness and generosity evident, thus stimulating growth in people. It's more though than a pot of jam we're referring to; it's the care invested in the natural processes of life and your things. You save to stimulate growth in yourself or those around you, and to bring quality to life at home. Growth comes from the rain you hear falling on your windows and from the pieces of cardboard and material on your table that a group of children are using for creative handicrafts. That's something to treasure.

✍ **Exercise 4**

Household objects are there to serve you while they move along with the stream of life at home. Where do things flow to your satisfaction and where do pile-ups occur? Is it the ironing or a cluttered hallway?

Sit down and do your job as household manager. There are certain jams or back-ups in your business. How can the problems be solved? Make a plan. Keep it in mind, write it down or express it in a colourful drawing.

Get outside advice; this could be from a neighbour, sister-in-law, friend or professional household advisor. Invite them to take a look at your venture and tell you what they've observed. You might even show them your plan. You can read more books on the subject.

In the end you'll be left with an assignment. Consider the solutions until your goal is clear (give yourself enough time). Before you know it, things will fall into place and matters will move in a new direction. You'll clear the back-up. Practice your decision for forty days and then ... celebrate! Stop complaining about cramped cupboards and do what needs to be done. Give yourself some space.

An encyclopedia contains facts and pictures, and is useful for a school project or to solve a problem, and aids growth. Growth is reflected in increased vocabulary, more precise words, progress, improving life and finding depth. The growth process is connected to the future, and relates to aspiration and the unexpected. Therefore, the best reason for keeping something is an affirmative answer to the question: "Can this help someone's growth?"

Reproduction

Finally, we reproduce. We create new life. One and one equals three, when two beings create a third. There are organs for this purpose in our bodies. The organism as a whole is nourished for sustenance and is therefore able to create new life. What about a household? Does it produce anything? Does it also procreate?

Think about home crafts, things you share, and beans that are planted and cultivated in your own garden. A plant produces more seeds than are needed to perpetuate the species. A grain field yields more grain than it takes to plant the next field, so there's plenty to grind into flour for making bread. What do you share with others from your household? Do you bring a gift from home to give your host when you visit? Do you make a pan of soup for your neighbours during a move? Do you bake biscuits for your nephew's birthday party? Do you paint a picture or play music to comfort a friend who has just been through a divorce? These are examples that come to mind when I think of sharing your own "surplus." You literally or figuratively offer nourishment to another's life. We speak of "raising" in connection with both crops and children. With the latter, this is an activity where all sorts of nourishment are given, so that children have enough in store to last throughout their lives. We give them a surplus to share with others.

The hospitality that I spoke of in Chapter One is also a household skill. This is something I experienced personally after the death of my first husband. It was so good to be welcomed and to eat or drink something with a caring family. It's a wonderful thing to be the recipient of hospitality. A surplus can transcend material matters; it's a product of those who have gone through their own growth process. These are people who offer nourishment to the world around them.

✍ **Exercise 5**

Treat your belongings with respect. Use them to their best advantage and store them in places that make the most sense.

Do you have migrating objects? What are they? List them in writing. Where do you use them most frequently? Can you create a home for them? Try to prepare a home base and put them there when you clean up. Tell your housemates and family members where they go. If necessary, label the spot with a sticker or something else. Keep at it for a few weeks.

The seven processes which I've described — consumption, warming-up, digestion, making choices, saving, growth and development, and reproduction — are physiological concepts; living processes. The first one is consuming food for your own well-being. We then move on through these processes, finally reaching the phase of giving nourishment to sustain someone else. I've drawn an analogy with household objects and how they nourish and travel through a household. The route they follow through your home and your life, as I've illustrated, is up to you. You are the one who moves your things from one process to the next. If they come to a standstill for too long, then what I call a jam develops. Space is lost at that spot, and just like a dammed river, the river banks become flooded. Empty space simply vanishes. It's as if breathing space is lacking when there's too much in one place. I'm often told that a tidy house is like a breath of fresh air; it's invigorating and creates new possibilities.

A young man was about to finish a college degree. Almost! He only had to write his thesis. Aside from this, he was webmaster of a skating site, organized excursions and babysat once a week for a friend's little boy. There wasn't much time left for his thesis. Getting around to tidying up was another stumbling block. Moreover, life outside the house was much more appealing than life inside it.

He asked me to assist him with organization. We started by cleaning up his living room/study/bedroom. We stripped the bed, put laundry in the laundry basket; unblocked the drain, washed the dishes and collected the empty bottles. All of his papers were placed on two piles on the table and the floor was cleared. We couldn't have asked for more. He resolved, from then on, to keep the room tidy by allotting an hour a day for that purpose. He timed it with a stopwatch, and only stopped working when the time was up. His room remained tidy; so tidy in fact that he even asked his mother to visit. The thesis has since been finished. He alternated his writing between the library and his table at home.

Full and empty, crowded and spacious, thick and thin — these are all contrasts. They need to be balanced in your own way, both in your home and your life. Balance is anything but static. Think of the concept of balance as scales, first tipping one way and then the other. Cleaning up is an exercise in balance. It's an art and you can learn its techniques. Read on.

To Have and to Hold

How things are acquired and how to give them a place

Let's take a closer look at the first and second processes mentioned in Chapter Three — consumption and warming-up. We will discuss how things enter your household and the places they end up in your house and your life.

Letting Things Enter

Things enter your home in many different ways. For example, through buying, receiving, picking up, inheriting, finding, borrowing and by making them yourself. I've selected a few to discuss.

Buying
You bring things into your home from outside, via the shopping bag from the stores where you've shopped. What do you actually do in those stores?

Do you usually have a shopping list with you and do you buy the items listed? Or are you someone who shops by playing it by ear? Evidence shows that going shopping directly after a meal contributes to buying less than shopping with a growling stomach. You must also realize that the displays in just about every store — whether for cheese,

✓ TIP

Publications from consumer organizations can be an inspiration for cutting down on consumption. There are periodicals in the United States, which promote frugal living such as "The Tightwad Gazette."

dresses or TVs — are presented as enticingly as possible. Merchandise is there for the grabbing, at hand or eye level. Are you easily tempted by attractive colours, bargains or free offers? Do you actually want to come home with all of the stuff that you've bought? Stores are designed to stimulate buying. Acquisition is in, consumption feels good and riches are desirable.

In 1987, before the implementation of free trade, I went to Moscow for two weeks. All of the shops were state-run and everyone was employed by the state. I didn't encounter any legitimate entrepreneurs. To buy a tube of toothpaste I had to go into a shop and join the queue. After a long wait, I finally arrived at a counter with a glass showcase. In it was a sample of each available item. After making my choice I pointed to the one I wanted. The woman who stood behind the counter wrote down my order on a piece of paper. With paper in hand I was directed to the next queue, which led me to the cash register. After waiting patiently, I handed the paper to the cashier and paid. I was then sent back to the first queue with the receipt and order. After yet another wait, the woman at the counter took the order and receipt, compared them and got the product. It was handed over to me and I was finally able to leave the shop with a tube of Russian toothpaste.

There was nothing particularly interesting about my buying behaviour in this shop. And the course of events didn't exactly inspire me to overdo it. It was a different story however on the street near my hotel, where a lively black-market in caviar and currency was operating to pro-cure foreign money.

In our society shopping is considered to be an outing or entertainment. It's a way of checking out new trends, escaping from work and home, doing some anonymous browsing or just unwinding in a cafe with a magazine. This is not just shopping; it's a lifestyle, to create an image and identity. At least that what those who work in marketing and advertising tell us.

Imagine that you're in a store full of things you feel compelled to buy. Consider the image of food entering the body of a living creature. Do your shopping bags resemble the wide-open mouths of birds eager to be fed? Is your house really that hungry? Do you even know what is really needed at home?

One of my students discovered that she often found herself going to the store, just for the sake of buying. She left home to go shopping when she felt bored, and a shop was where she found what was lacking! A new purchase can create a high. She discovered that she had unanswered needs, but on an immaterial level. She suffered no lack of material objects, but experienced a shortage of satisfaction just the same. A discussion was then triggered in class about buying goods, services (a hairdresser's or a plumber's), experience (an expert in white-water rafting), and distraction (an entertainment industry product or going out). The discussion made us realize how fed up we were with buying for the sake of it. We ended the lesson talking about all the wonderful things that only cost time and energy. We came up with: socializing over a cup of tea; a long meaningful conversation; playing cards with an older relative; taking time out to sit in the park enjoying the birds; and putting a model farm together with a children. You might also consider other challenges such as new studies, learning to play the

The spoon (1)

I taught games in an elementary school for six years. I'd been observing a few of the older boys and couldn't believe my eyes. They were about twelve years old and spent most of their time hanging out on the street, constantly distributing sweets among themselves, and I once had the opportunity to see how they acquired it, while standing behind them in line at the store. One of the boys put a bag of sweets on the checkout counter to pay and when the cashier looked at him suspiciously, the boy responded: "If you don't trust me, you can check my pockets." This didn't happen and the boy left the store. Once outside, it appeared that he had two additional bags hidden on him, after all, which he shared with the others. I confronted him with what I'd seen and went home with the incident still on my mind. I decided to shoplift to find out how it would affect me. I went to a store selling household articles, put a spoon in my pocket and left without paying. The high I felt from stealing was a completely different one than buying. My heart was racing a mile a minute.

piano, voluntary work, a reading group, getting involved in politics or community service.

Needs and fulfilment go together like hand and glove. If you purchase the wrong glove, the fit's not right and your hand will feel cramped or cold. Buying brings things into your home. These won't serve you if they're not contributing to help a real need. Are you what you buy? I don't believe so. It takes more than material goods and economics to define people. There are more aspects to life. It's truly an art to discover your talents, express yourself, and help others to do the same. It's an undertaking that can last a lifetime.

Consumption, such as buying new things, can be an expression of individuality.

Decide beforehand how much, or how little, you want. Your standards are your own. To maintain your health you watch your intake of food and drink. Similarly, your household has a quota all its own. Try leaving a store empty-handed, if you realize that you went there for something other than a lack of goods. Enjoy the coat you recently bought to the utmost. If it's really some-

 TIP

Using the services of a colour advisor or a stylist can help to prevent poor buys. I have had good personal experience with both. Their advice has given me more insight into the colours, which match my complexion, and styles which suit my figure. This can also help you to develop a taste of your own.

thing you have a use for, then the basis for a good relationship has been established with your coat. My old tent had been damaged for quite some time and following an extensive search for a new one and many catalogues later, I finally put it out of mind. While shopping for a new rain cape with a friend, I saw the ideal tent on display right there in the camping store. It was just waiting to enter my life, and I knew it was meant for me. Sometimes we sense these things. That tent, now in my possession, has since accompanied me many times on camping trips to Lapland, Switzerland, Denmark and France. It was a good purchase and is still a source of great pleasure.

I wonder if people in Europe can even imagine being happy without material goods. They think we're all miserable, here in Pampas, because we have to do without. Just being together makes us happy.
    Karin Jesusi, from the slums of Pampas, Lima, Peru.

Now that everyone is satiated with material belongings, products are aimed more at people's immaterial needs.

We want to experience the extraordinary in our scarce free time, and therefore go to pop concerts and amusement parks.
> Jeroen Duijvenstein, *Jonas* magazine.

The kick from buying is definitely as important as the use of the object itself.
> Gertjan van Schoonhoven, *Elsevier* magazine.

Aside from their function (a raincoat is waterproof), things have an image (the brand of the raincoat also says something about your taste, choice of lifestyle). Images are easily changed and this keeps the cash flowing.
> David Brooks, *Bobo's in Paradise.*

Make sure that you don't have more than you can care for.
> Henry David Thoreau.

Receiving and Inheritance

Inheriting and receiving hand-me-downs are different from buying goods. Things that belonged to someone else enter your daily life, but what are they doing there? Do they add value or are they superfluous? How do you relate to the emotional value of these things, or to the story that accompanies them? They can bring on feelings of appreciation, which may be warranted. Qualities such as technical excellence, the exquisite structure of wooden objects, craftsmanship, artful design, fair trade, ecological considerations, or the history of a piece of furniture, all deserve our respect. Care about your things! If you do, you will want to treat them well so that they last a long time. Maybe they're meant to exist in your home, though it's also a possibility that a particular cupboard would be better in a different place.

That can be accomplished through an auction, an advert or another method. Looking for a suitable new home demonstrates your interest in the object's future existence.

Suggested by Wim Verjaal, but yet to be entered into the Dictionary:

House weeds *(noun)*. All sorts of items that through devious means penetrate an interior and lead a persistent, yet useless, existence there.

A friend, who had recently moved there, told me about a tradition practiced in a Dutch province, which I've heard is customary in other places as well. I'm referring to "granting." People who are looking for a house through a real estate agent, are invited to meet the owners. Though price is certainly an issue in the buying and selling process, the owner's understanding that you show respect for the house also plays a role. If she recognizes this, you are *granted* the house. This tradition is connected with the concept of caring. The former owner can feel such a strong bond with her house and garden that she's not able to grant it to just anybody who comes along. I think it's remarkable that "granting" and "caring about something" also have a function in economic activity.

Borrowing

Borrowing is a form of temporary consumption. It's a common practice with books. If you borrow a book and read it — thus making its acquaintance — you have it on trial. When you've had enough of it you return it to its owner or to the library. If you enjoyed it you may want to prolong the relationship, in which case you can find a shop that sells it, and buy a copy for yourself.

Renting is increasingly popular and shows that people may

want to, or do, relate to the things they use with less commitment than ownership requires. Not everyone is prepared to spend the time on caring, repairing and storage that possession calls for.

Welcoming Things

Once things have entered your life they are in your keeping. One object is useful to you and you love another for its beauty, so you give each a place in your home. You put apples in the fruit bowl and your new lipstick with the other make-up items. As a rule, if you put things where they're used they will probably stay put. For example, the phonebook's place is near the phone and the stamps are kept with the envelopes. Having your things logically located promotes a smooth-running household.

> **✓ Tip**
>
> Pick up things that you come across daily but practically never use. Look for an attic-like spot for storage. Keep your living areas tidy and roomy.

Six years ago, I stayed with friends in the Gambia for three weeks. They lived in a compound composed of a circle of loam huts with straw roofs. The village was made up of many such compounds. In the hut next door a woman called "Mama Isathou" lived with her grandson, Ousman, who was still at school. His father lived opposite them and worked to earn money. On reaching adulthood it's customary there for a young man to leave home and receive a hut from the village. Sometimes an empty one is available, sometimes a new one is built specially, or the young man builds it himself. They thus receive, as a start to their adult life, a home, a base, their very own spot. I thought this was an

✍ Exercise 6

Pick a spot in your house and sit down there. Look around the chosen room and take notice of the things there, and think of how they got there: acquired, bought, harvested, inherited, found, planted, subscribed to — there are infinite possibilities. Concentrate on one spot; it could be a windowsill, table or a shelf in a cupboard. Copy the list below into a notebook (add the headings that apply) and examine the things you've taken notice of according to the heading they fall under.

Acquired   Bought   Inherited   Found   Planted   Subscribed

....

You've now listed how things have entered your home. Is there something that strikes you in particular about your list? In my case, the first and second headings were equally long, which was a huge realization.

Concentrate one by one on the bought items on the list and ask yourself: Was the purchase impulsive or well-considered? Was it satisfactory or do I regret it? Was I lured into buying the object, or did I know what I wanted? Lastly, do I or don't I enjoy having it in my home at this moment?

Look at the items in the column of acquired and inherited things. Who did it come from and when did I get it? What does it contribute to my life?

With regard to the *found* items, we especially appreciate them in the beginning — a number of pretty pink seashells from a trip to the beach adorn the windowsill for a while — but as time goes by they start to lose your attention, and the shells start collecting dust. Be aware of the moment this happens, so the shells can make way for something new. They might serve their purpose in the garden; a scrapbook certainly wouldn't be an option but the compost heap is perfect.

If you feel that you have too many things and you want to do something about it, this can promote insight into your own consumption behaviour. You'll be more aware at the moments you consume.

excellent idea; one that should be applied to people from all walks of life. Simply because you've been born, you're permitted a place of your own. Following a day of being outdoors, after work or school, you can return to your own home. You can relax on your own or be with others. It's yours, in good times and times of hardship. Everyone deserves his or her place in the sun.

This is the same attitude I hold with regard to the objects in a house. Since they're there, they deserve a home base. You know where to find them when you need them, and you put them in the same spot again when you tidy up. Otherwise, you are faced with a short circuit. Keys, cards, addresses and scissors have a special talent for being misplaced, and have a knack of hiding among old papers behind a cupboard. They're often the cause of much inconvenience by being where they don't belong.

I recently bought a newspaper in which a woman named Ada Jonkman related how she made a decision to take off and leave when she was about thirty years old. She travelled through France and Spain and wrote a book about her experiences. After ten years of drifting she longed for stability and a place of her own. Together with her boyfriend she was able to rebuild her life. She wrote:

> "The good thing about having a roof over your head is that we are now able to grow; we now have the opportunity to get things done. When you're drifting, everything is in such a state of uncertainty that you don't undertake anything new."

Thinking about the concept, "a place of your own" can help you to view the objects *adrift* in your home from a new perspective. Can you find them a good home base, so that they can fulfil the function for which they were brought home?

A worker had been at home since May as a result of stress-related illness and had received no word whatsoever from his boss or colleagues. At Christmas they sent him a Christmas bouquet, which he considered tasteless. He deposited it in the garbage and wrote in response: "Thanks for your attention, I've put it in the appropriate place."

An acquaintance told me that much of her clothing is black and that she can never find what she's looking for. She finds it easier to go to a shop and buy something new than locate the right blouse for a jacket that she can't seem to find, but she thinks this buying policy is far from satisfactory. She could improve the situation by organizing an appropriate place to keep her clothes, where she has a good overview of her skirts, trousers and blouses, where they're practically arranged for finding and trying on.

As soon as things are in your home they're your responsibility, though it's not always easy to accept something new. Newly-acquired items are not always ours for the choosing. What do you do with that awful vase you were given for your birthday? How do you *warm things up* and when shouldn't you even bother?

Energy plays a role in the process of making something really yours. Does an object have an energy that's good for you, or is it a source of irritation? Do you want to keep it or would you rather get rid of it? If you allow too many "cold" objects in your house, caring is bound to diminish. This results in a decrease of energy. Moreover, in time, your cupboards become clogged with meaningless items, with which you have no relationship. Receiving unwanted things from well-meaning people can be the source of conflicted feelings. You can however accept the gesture while letting go of an unwanted vase.

One person will get rid of everything that doesn't give

✍ Exercise 7

Stand in your hallway. What kind of a place is it? What was its original purpose and what would you like to do with it?

A hall is the place where life outdoors is exchanged for life indoors and vice versa; it's an area of transition. What are the necessary conditions to ensure that a place of this type can function properly? A spot for shoes and slippers and a coat rack for hanging jackets come to mind. I want hooks for my bags, a key rack for my various sets of keys, and of course a mirror to make sure my hair looks good. Look around your hall and ask yourself if the items you see enhance your "hall life." Is there an excess of something, or is something lacking? Do you see *migrating* objects?

With pen and paper to hand approach all the rooms in your home in this way. This will help you to establish your wishes and clean-up chores. If you find yourself with a really long list, just write down your observations. You can put them in a logical sequence at a later point, before getting on with the job.

This exercise will help you to find a sensible home base for your things. However, please keep one thing in mind: if your house is too small or not suitably constructed, you'll have to make compromises. It's especially helpful to go through your house with your partner or a friend in the way described above. It's highly recommended and fun to do!

The following comments are from students after doing this exercise:

— "I've arranged a lot of places more logically and now have two extra empty cupboards and an empty shelf."

— "I've noticed that giving my things a place of their own makes a real difference in dealing with unmanageable chaos."

pleasure to him or her; another saves things for the sake of loyalty and tries to appreciate what's been received; a third gives it a couple of weeks or months and then makes a decision; and the fourth doesn't have a clue and just puts it anywhere. What's the best policy? Is it keeping only the things that give off good energy? The last option illustrates the view of Karen Kingston, in *Unclutter your home with Feng Shui.*

If I look around the room where I am sitting and writing I can see a mug, which I received from a neighbourhood friend when we were fifteen years old. I'm not wild about it, nor was I then, but I've kept it, despite many moves. That girl and I didn't always get along, but we persevered and always resolved our differences. Resilience and endurance in relationships are recurrent themes in my personal history, and that mug exemplifies this.

So one thing stays while another makes a quick exit. When in doubt I would advise you to make a subjective choice. Warming things up means that they reach your "temperature" and this means in turn that you reach theirs.

I can already hear the protests concerning a certain chair

The Spoon (2)

The stolen spoon ended up in a holder with other spoons and stayed there for a while. No one ever took it out arbitrarily or otherwise! It was useless; it didn't participate in daily living. Then a friend told me that he liked it so I gave it to him (cowardly in hindsight). I thought I'd put the incident behind me, but this apparently wasn't so. I would have liked to do something about it. I realized then and there that honesty is the best policy; at least it is for me. Something dishonestly acquired doesn't contribute to my home life.

that you'd like to see the back of, but about which your partner categorically disagrees. This calls for consultation. Discuss the warming aspect and aim for a win-win solution that satisfies you both. It might mean that the chair needs to be sanded down and refinished; it might need re-upholstering or a new location in your home. It could also mean that one of you chooses to tolerate it. No one said it's easy, but it's certainly not worth a domestic crisis. Have a good talk. Even a chair as a starting point can be revealing.

To Save or Discard?

Decision-making and goal fulfilment

If we had X-ray vision and could see through cupboards and walls, how would the objects inside appear? Imagine how the cutlery lies together, how scarves are stacked in a box and how trousers hang from a hanger on a bar, visible only to us. Now and then a hand grasps for something inside an open drawer or cupboard; the thing, which is taken, participates in the life of a person living in that house. For the things in question, wearing out, being eaten or given away are consequences of participation — things await their utilization.

A painting is hung to be looked at and a bowl of apple sauce waits to be eaten. Objects exist for our use. Imagine that you're planning on taking a hike the following weekend. You search for the items you will need. You look for appropriate walking shoes and socks, a thermos flask for coffee, and a backpack to put it in. You might also look for a bird guide, binoculars and waterproofs. You gather this stuff from various nooks and crannies for the purpose of the hike. Your things are an aid to fulfilling wishes. That's what they are for.

We live with the objects in our homes. Some of them are used every day, such as toothbrushes or pens. Others, like Christmas decorations, maps, and ice skates might be used once a year or less. Objects have their own "rhythms of use."

✓ Tip

Do you save out of courtesy? Did you once receive a set of crockery that you don't really like and you almost never use? Take it out of the cupboard and put it in the attic. Courtesy and loyalty could be reasons for keeping things but what are reasonable terms? Would you wait a year or even ten to make a decision?

Think about this "act of keeping". Choose a period of time and forget about the item until the designated period has passed. When the time comes you can reconsider and decide what's best.

There are also things that are never used. You may have lost your taste for them; they may be broken, forgotten or covered with dust. They no longer participate in your life — their rhythm is out of sync.

Unused things, those that you no longer care about, those that lie around or those you have to do something with (at some undefined point), we refer to as *junk*. Junk has a remarkable talent for patient waiting. Every time you pass it you feel a faint gnawing, and that feeling can deplete energy. A backlog of chores sucks your energy drop-by-drop. I see this in people who procrastinate in tackling their own backlog. It can even lead to apathy.

If this is the case, we usually turn our backs on these chores and find loads of excuses not to do them. My advice is: Transform the situation and get them done.

And now for some more advice in the form of a riddle: How do you eat an elephant?

Answer: A little bit at a time. My motto is thus, "work on it." The time that a job takes can be split up into, for instance, units of an hour. For example: Clean up one bookshelf per week. This is more satisfying than weeks of dreading having to deal with an entire bookcase. Work through the job consistently, one small task after another, until it's done, but make sure it gets finished. The pressure will be off and you'll feel relief. Cross the chore off your list; look back with satisfaction at what you've accomplished; take a week's break and start again by splitting up a new job into phases.

Dealing with an overdue clean-up job needs time; it also needs energy and some organizational ability. How do you tackle a long-standing job?

> ✔ TIP
>
> If you feel a strong resistance towards cleaning up, start with a simple chore, a kitchen shelf, for instance. Reward yourself. Don't be put off if you create even more chaos by tackling the job. Ask yourself, item by item, if it benefits your life. If the answer is yes, then put it back. If it's no, take it to your departure point.

A woman and I cleaned her desk together one morning in May. The clutter on her desk, which had developed into a mountainous pile, had been bothering her since the previous November. We started by placing an empty table nearby — an ironing board would do. Each item was transferred from the desk to the table. Every drawer and compartment was emptied. We then cleaned what turned out to be a lovely piece of furniture, and placed her chair in front of it.

Sitting at her empty desk she took each bundle as I handed it to her. The stamps went in the stamp drawer and we tried out each pen. Paper for recycling was put in a pile. She put her son's swimming certificate with his belongings. There were nostalgic objects, papers for her husband, unfinished administrative work, and a huge supply of envelopes. The piles to dispose of grew larger and the table was quickly cleared. We tied up all the loose ends and before we knew it, forty minutes had gone by. The mountain she had feared for the past six months had shrunk considerably. What was she actually doing while sitting

✓ T<small>IP</small>

When cleaning up an entire house, it's best to start with the sheds, garages and attics, if you have them. These future storage and departure areas will then be ready for use.

at her desk that morning? Was it really cleaning up? What energy was required? She was constantly asking herself: "Is this meant to be in our house, or somewhere else?" "Do I keep it or throw it away?" Every item that she held was subject to a choice.

Cleaning up means making choices. If you find this difficult then limit the time to, let's say, thirty minutes; take a break and then continue. If you definitely want to keep something, put it where it belongs. If you still don't have a definite spot, then make that your next project. Those items definitely pegged for disposal should be taken to the door, so they can then be taken to their final destination the same week. Create a departure area in your house; this is the spot in which you put the things you've chosen to get rid of. They then only need to be taken away. This is also the place for old paper and returnable bottles. Don't forget about a special spot for outgoing mail. Your departure area is also the place for borrowed things, which need to be returned, shopping lists and the birthday present that needs to be delivered. It is comparable to a departure hall at an airport; and can be a lively area that settles down in time, before the buzzing picks up again. That's the nature of the place.

In the case of items you might feel hesitant about, one option is to have a spot designated for "dubious items." This way, you allow yourself time to consider. Be sure though to remove these uncertain items from their normal places to avoid being confronted by them on a daily basis. This way you'll discover their significance in your household. Within a week, or even a month, you'll know if you've missed them and you'll have a better idea as to what you should do with them. My own spot for dubious items is the boot of my car. I keep a crate there for these things and those I aim to sell or trade. Sometimes I give away something in the crate, and other times I take an object out and bring it back inside. There are scores of possibilities lying in that crate and chance conversations with others help me to make the right choices.

Quotes from students following a three month clean-up campaign:

— Letting things go costs energy and is liberating.
— I can't make decisions continuously for more than an hour at a stretch.
— I clean up if I feel "I can make choices today."
— I can't get myself to clean up every time I have a free moment. I also need time to relax; I need time to let the clean-up job settle within me. I tackle a job spontaneously, and I enjoy doing it.

You give a household its individual mood by choosing between keeping or discarding. This creates an opportunity to run a really personal household, where you can truly feel at home. Would you rather put aside money for a dishwasher or wash your dishes by hand? You give shape to your own style of living, as well as to the organization of your cupboards and the arrangement of the rooms in your home, through the choices you make.

Some people are unaware of their own personal style of living and a long process might be involved before even starting to understand what it

 TIP

Besides cutting down on the amount of things you have, you can also reduce your activity load. Getting organized takes place both internally and externally.

You'll need a blank piece of paper, pencil and crayons. Write the words "my life" in the middle of the paper. Write down all your activities around these words according to the category. Draw a line from the middle of the paper to each category, so that you will have made a *map* of the different areas in your life — it should resemble a sun with beams. Include your not-yet-fulfilled, dormant wishes. Some of the areas that apply to you might not be tangible; for instance, spiritual or religious experience. Some people are active thinkers. (see page 110).

Put your map away for a day. Afterwards adjust it as you see fit. Ask yourself how you feel about each of your areas. Are you satisfied with matters concerning a hobby? Do you want to spend more time on something and less on something else? Colour the lines of the work-related areas blue; housework, green; social activities, yellow; and the things you do purely for yourself, red. If you prefer to use other colours, that's fine, but try not to use more than six. This will help you to see your landscape clearly. Circle the areas which are most important to you.

Sleep on it overnight and when you pick up the exercise again, ask yourself the following questions: Do you have appropriate resources to back up these important areas? I would include photo albums, birth and wedding announcements, saved correspondence and obituaries with regard to the area "family and friends." How have you stored these objects and are they easily accessible? A special shelf in the cupboard comes to mind, for poetry volumes, which you've been meaning to spend more time reading.

The last step. We've spoken about "goal fulfilment." You save things for the purpose of accomplishing something. Take another look at these areas and save what is realistic, and right for you, and what will help you fulfil your goals.

The emergent clean-up chores are significant to your life, and are directly connected to the themes of your being. You could ask yourself what all the other objects in your household are doing there. Do they fit in to your life? If they participate in the lives of your partner, children or other housemates, they fall under their care. If your children are still small, you must fill in temporarily.

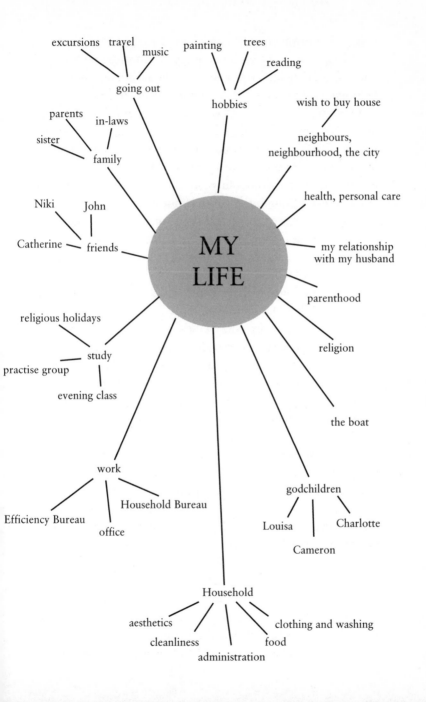

may be. However, through daily living, answers can be found, or you might look for advice from those with experience. Deciding on how you want your home, and on the belongings kept there, is all part of the art of living.

I recommend Exercise 8 to practice "goal fulfilment." Just as we keep our belongings, so we aim to keep our promises. Do we stick to our resolutions and keep goals in mind? Which ones are important enough to keep? Having an idea about the course you follow in life can help you to make choices, even though the route is not always obvious.

Hopefully this exercise will shed some light on the subject and help bring perspective into your life. However, perspective is hard to achieve with a head full of chaos. I often do these exercises when giving a course or doing personal coaching. My experience is that people make meaningful discoveries while doing the exercises. This is especially true when you're able to compare your "landscape" with that of another.

You can balance the reasons for keeping or discarding things against one other. When I speak of "discarding" I mean *removing* items from your household. This doesn't necessarily imply throwing things in the bin. Selling or giving away is also an option. How much are you keeping because you don't want to throw it away, but don't know what to do about it either?

It's also possible that the amount you possess is reasonable, but you are unable to store it. In that case, you don't have too many things, but lack storage space.

Start your pursuit for more cupboards only after you have a clear idea what you need to store. That way, you'll have a better idea which type suits your needs. Maybe you'd prefer an alternative to free-standing cupboards or cabinets, which can take up a lot of living space.

Low cupboards, however, take up less space than high ones and those with doors give more illusion of order than open cupboards. Unburden the living-area and other spaces where you spend a lot of time. Whenever possible it's prefer-

> *A client's reaction:*
> I was feeling discontented; I needed to do something else with my life, but I didn't know what — not to mention the lack of space to undertake anything, due to the chaos. When I finally started to clean up, it became obvious to me what I wanted to do with my life.

able to organize an attic or attic-like space for efficient storage. Don't forget a practical system for finding things again.

When something has been used and approved we *keep* it. Jopie Huisman lived in the Dutch province of Friesland, and was what we call a *ragman;* he collected old clothes. In other words, he gathered things that others had used until they no longer had use for them. Jopie could see the life-story of his old town through a pair of second-hand shoes. He loved these old things and sketched them. There's a museum in the province filled with his drawings. Every one of the objects he drew had a long life behind it; they spent a long time with real people, and became aged, emitting wisdom.

> Tying up loose ends and putting your things in a suitable place helps to bring a healthy tempo to a hectic life.

Using something for a good purpose brings satisfaction. Every house contains objects both new and old; for example, in my house there is a painting created in the year 2000. Near it stands a silver candelabrum that's about seventy years old, that came from my grandfather's house, and which has been with me for twenty years. Once while polishing it, it occurred to me that this object is older than I am, and will most likely outlive me. If I allow the history of an object to penetrate my thoughts, many reflections come to mind. I also observe this in my students. Following a summer of tidying I heard the following comments:

— Is what I've been doing all these years what I really want to do?
— Can I discover what I really want?
— If I could do it over again, this time I'd borrow those books and magazines. Possessions make me feel claustrophobic.
— Sometimes an old hobby is over and done with. I've auctioned off all my knitting things and wool via the internet.
— When my new boyfriend moves in, I'm going to clear out a room to give him space.
— I've discovered where there's too much "old," too little "new" can enter.
— Now that I know that I do have respect for things, discarding them has become easier. This gives me empowerment.
— We don't want to get rid of anything. The attic and shed are now efficiently organized, which gives me peace of mind.
— I sometimes need a ritual to discard old things. I want to be able to contemplate when a phase in my life comes to an end.

✔ TIP

Farewell suitcase
I've discovered that a number of my clients have a case full of belongings for use in the event of their death. What are the contents? Think about a will, life insurance policy, phone numbers of the family doctor, and close family and friends. The names and addresses of people you want to attend the funeral can also be included.

I read a magazine article about a woman who had saved a great deal during her life, and was grateful for both the life she'd lived as well as her things. It so happened that her neighbour broke a hip and was no longer able to live at home, so the house was cleared out and sold. The woman observed how passers-by would stop to look and rummage through her neighbour's rejected possessions on the street. It was a distressing sight. Five years later, she was still in the process of reducing her effects, and was able to discard a lot via advertisements and the Salvation Army. She prepared a suitcase with personal belongings meant for her two grown-up sons. There was certainly a sad note to this farewell, but it was important to her that the decision was her own.

We've discussed making your household personal to you. Will I use this thing sometime in the future with pleasure, or would I rather have the space it takes up, in that future? Keeping is something we do with future usage in mind, or discarding, with future space in mind. What's your choice?

Another example from my experience: I cleaned a house with a client as she was unable to see her way through the job. We started by making a layout for her attic, and she even went so far as to hang a sketch of the plan on the door, which helped her to be consistent about tidying each time she went to the attic. We also tackled the bedroom and even washed the windows to literally "make it shine" after finishing the job. We encountered quite a few dubious items in bags, cupboards and boxes, which often fell into the category of pieces of material and hand-made dresses, but there were none that she was willing to discard. Could something be made from the material? What about the dresses? True, they no longer fitted, but if she lost some weight ...

While discussing things we hung the outgrown dresses on hangers on a rack in the attic. Many memories were hanging there together, seventeen to be exact, and now that they were in the open these items acted as a catalyst — to keep or discard ... We left them hanging, each with our own thoughts regarding the outcome.

Order was restored to her house following our tidying project. She has since started studying music. She enjoys what she's doing and has plans to start a career in this field. She no longer has any interest in unread newspapers and has less trouble throwing them out. Her church organized a clothes drive for Eastern Europe and she donated her seventeen dresses without regret. It took her six months to realize that what had been hanging from the rack in the attic, was merely an illusion. I heard that the pieces of material are still there. Who knows, maybe another chapter will yet be added to their story.

When there's a major emotional attachment to certain items it's best to give yourself time. A decision regarding keeping or discarding can only take place when you feel detached from these things; it's more of an internal organization of past life occurrences than just a practical chore. Sometimes psychotherapy can be more useful than a clean-up plan. Work on your mind-set and exchange ideas with others. Life itself can offer solutions.

> ✓ TIP
>
> During a major clean-up have boxes and bags ready. You can always assess what you have after sorting everything out, and then make the decision to save or discard. Finding a good destination helps in the discarding process. Use the empty boxes to categorize the items to be taken away — clothing, usable blankets, tools, unused toys, garage sale items etc. Each one has an appropriate destination. Use a felt-tip to write the contents on the outside of the box.

If you encounter similar situations during a major clean-up project, then I think it's wise not to try to tackle them extensively, but to set them aside. The project will lose too much momentum otherwise. Choose a moment to cope with things of this nature when you have more time and the serenity to handle it. Hold on to them as long as you need in order to come to terms with them.

My first husband passed away and every year on the anniversary of his death I take a day off. I've been doing this now for the past sixteen years. It's become a commemoration of sorts and every year I observe it differently, and every year I experience different feelings.

One of the things I do that day is go through his belongings

Food for thought

Eliminating belongings can take some time. Others don't always want what you're giving away. You have to become familiar with the second-hand circuit. Reactions to advertisements don't come overnight. The satisfaction received from tying up loose ends is your reward. There's something indifferent about simply throwing things away; this is a common feeling, especially where functional items are concerned.

It's odd that nobody thinks twice about taking the time to look for a suitable travel bag or waiting for a new bed to be delivered, yet when discarding items we want fast results. This makes the waiting involved that much harder. Finding appropriate new destinations demands care and attention. Practising this will have an effect on your future buying; you'll develop a better understanding of what's involved with caring for things: "Let's limit the grocery shopping, so there won't be so much to clean up afterwards." You gain experience by purchasing and therefore have more insight into what happens to you by making a certain purchase; you can then judge better if it's something you want to undertake.

and over time they have diminished considerably. As the years pass, many of his personal belongings have gone to others, at my own pace and in my own fashion. A box with photographs and letters and a box of pastels, which I use occasionally, still remains.

Good excuses
I bet you've got a few of your own:

I'm going to keep this. All these books give me status.
This coat was much too expensive; I was sorry the moment, I bought it, but I can't get rid of it.
My mother did it this way too.
My house will be so empty
What will I do without these things?
I'll only throw it away if I get something else instead.
It's part of the scenery here.

Another story from my experience:

The house of a woman client of mine seemed roomy enough, and she lived there with her husband and three children. The result of our tour through the house was a list of tidying activities. Everywhere we went we found unused things scattered among the things used every day. Despite this, I had the impression that the job could be accomplished within a reasonable time frame. I was in the process of saying goodbye, when I mentioned how lucky she was to have a garage. My own car is always subject to the elements and hers can be parked inside. She gave me a look and took me to the garage's side door, and opened the door. The space was jam-packed. It was full of unused things such as a broken sofa, boxes of paper, bags filled with who-knows-what, planks, containers and various cupboards. I couldn't refrain from asking if she preferred giving shelter to a lot of old junk rather than to a good car. She glanced from me to

✍ **Exercise 9**

Make a similar list in your notebook based on your own experiences.

What keeps me from cleaning up? or	*What helps me to clean up?*
First I have to...	Just tackling it
I need for energy to do it	Doing a chore a week
I won't be able to maintain it	Starting with a job that gets direct results
Who cares about the piles of junk?	A friend is coming to help out
I did it before and it didn't help	Treating myself as soon as I'm finished
I have no clue where to begin	Making a list of chores and crossing off what's done
I only have an hour, so forget it	A friend in the same situation is calling on Saturday
I'm not dressed for the job	A friend and I do clean-up chores together, one week at her place, the next at mine
....	....
....	....
....	....
....	....

Food for thought

There are those who live their lives by always looking ahead; their main focus is the future. Items, which have hardly been used, are soon considered outdated. When a boss is in this situation his or her secretary is expected to sort out these things without delay. This type of person is continuously taking on something new. They want it all, and aren't inclined to give much attention to the here and now, not to mention, file maintenance.

The attitude of someone who'd rather look back is an entirely different story. This is a type who "feels a touch of sadness about that which has passed." This person is a collector and tends to go into detail about what "has been." Their interest is directed towards the origin of things and this lies at the foundation of their general outlook. Saving characterizes their way of life.

Of course you recognize the types described here. One of these descriptions must fit you.

The trouble with one-sidedness is that it means there's a loss of balance. If you recognize this problem you can counter balance your character. Exercising a new habit can help restore stability. You might try a clean-up hour once a month or every week, or a "letting go hour."

the car and then to the contents of the garage. I knew something had dawned on her by the look on her face. The job has since been accomplished and she now parks her car inside.

We are now approaching the next chapter. We've just completed the section about saving and eliminating. Eliminating means taking out of the house and saving means keeping within the house, but what does this require from you? We'll take a closer look in the following chapter.

The Art of Saving Things

The difference between storage and retrieval Systems

Who doesn't save things? You save something because you want to use or see it at a later point in time. Do you keep your resolutions? Is there a reasonable chance that you'll ever use the kept items again, or is it, in fact, an illusion that you'll use your light-weight backpack to go mountain climbing considering your bad knees? Will it ever really happen? Who knows, maybe one day that backpack will come in handy.

Fulfilling promises seems so mature. Living up to expectations, such as the promises and resolutions you've made, proves your reliability. It's often a struggle to stick to the commitments you've made, to fulfil them to the utmost, and on your uphill struggle to get there you may just wonder "What have I taken on?" Have you ever started to knit a jumper, and halfway through knitting the back, decided to make a vest instead, because the sleeves were too much work? If you consume a lot and take on a lot, you have a big load riding on your shoulders. All these responsibilities require care and action.

The ability to keep your promises is essential during the process of keeping or discarding. If the answer is yes, you keep something, and a decision has then been made. You accumulate a wealth of objects, which definitely participate in your household. They have been saved because you assume that at a certain moment they will contribute something worthwhile. When that moment arrives you want to find them in good condition.

Aspects of the art of saving include making sure that objects remain in good condition and that they can be found again. This chapter illustrates that you can work out for yourself how to save your things.

Food

What kind of things do we save? Most of us store food; whether the quantities happen to be large or small, we want it to keep well. Jam can be kept for years in glass jars if sterile and airtight. Our grandmothers canned fruit and vegetables in glass pots especially made for this purpose. Freezers have since emerged, and for many have become a place for food storage. Cellars and pantries also contain jars, potatoes and canned goods. Arrange them according to expiration date and don't forget to eat them now and then. You can also save things for too long, and having to throw things away is a waste of all the care that's been taken. Recipes and tips for proper storage can be found in cookbooks.

Clothing

How do you deal with clothing? Do you hang woollen jumpers outdoors to air in the spring? Do you keep your winter jumpers somewhere particular during the summer? I advise a summer-winter switch for three reasons:

Your everyday cupboards have more space. This is an advantage, and shouldn't be underestimated.

You go through your wardrobe twice a year and can take stock of what you have and what you may want to add. If you have children, you can go through their things, and remove items they have out-grown.

I'm always surprised in October and April when I switch my summer and winter things. "Hey, I'd completely forgotten about that." It's a greeting of sorts, and there's a feeling of appreciation for that item because I haven't seen it for six months.

If there are many bags in your house, or if you have numerous house-mates, write the bag owner's name on the bag. This helps if you need to find something in-between times. If you don't adopt

 TIP

My grandmother had a list with the contents of her linen cupboard hanging on the inside. Try it if you think it would help you.

the switch method described above, I advise finding your own rhythm, once or twice yearly, to go through and assess your wardrobe. At that point, remove everything from your cupboard, put back what you regularly wear, and make a pile of things to discard. Dubious items will remain. Put them back in the cupboard and if you find them unused the following year, you can make a decision then. This way, you have a conversation of sorts with your wardrobe. For one individual a quick chat will do; another person will get into involved and

---

✓ TIP

I've seen advice about eradicating ants, making a wood louse trap, herbs for moth and roach control and others in "Tips from Grandmothers" in the *Reader's Digest*. According to one grandmother, ants are gone for good if you place fresh tomato leaves or fresh chervil along their route. I believe they retreat to where they came from. Wood lice apparently have seven pairs of legs and are virtually harmless. You can lure them with a hollowed-out potato, into which they will crawl. You can then bring them — potato and all — to the compost heap, being both people- and environmentally-friendly at the same time.

A silverfish tip: Put a damp, white cotton cloth where you've spotted them, and sprinkle plaster on top. You'll find large quantities of these insects on the cloth the morning after. Take them to a place of no return and shake the cloth out. The book doesn't give directions for getting there.

---

repeated discussions. My advice is to act according to your character.

Moths, by the way, are not fond of airing, lavender flowers or scented soap. Newspapers between layers of clothing, red cedar chips and fresh springtime leaves from walnut trees are not big favourites either. It's best to call your local health department or professional exterminators for vermin such as mice, rats, cockroaches and termites. They can advise you and, if necessary, come with appropriate artillery.

Slow objects

An attic or similar space is the place to store "slow" objects. These are things that don't frequently "perform," but have a supporting role instead, and which contribute to your life.

Food for thought

If you've completed a clean-up operation, you've got good cause to be proud of yourself. Hestia herself would glance at your professionally organized hanging folder drawer with pleasure. We often lack appreciation and long for a reward, which is nothing to be ashamed of. Provide one for yourself, be proud and let somebody in on it. Be just as happy with your present to yourself as you would with a present from another.

This definitely applies to my camping equipment. It is also true of the contents in my Christmas crate. Both are important to my well-being. We may also save old curtains or perhaps a collection of wooden planks; boxes with semi-precious stones from childhood; a few un-hung paintings; a dismantled cupboard; old toys; rolls of wallpaper and carpet remnants for any eventuality …

Make sure items are saved for easy retrieval by putting them with similar objects. Craft and handiwork items belong together, so does electrical equipment. Things you're saving for your children for later on should be put in a particular corner, etc.

✔ TIP

Storage advice: Grandmothers and mothers are the experts. They appreciate you asking and it's a good way to perpetuate tradition.

Then, if you need something you'll only have to look for it in one place. Decision-making about appropriate storage spots for other objects brought to the attic is also then made easier. Sketch your floor plan and attach it to a beam. This will be a help to others in your house.

✔ TIP

Make a mail tray for each person. You can do this in the house or in the office. Always sort the mail straight into these trays.

Papers

The loudest groans are uttered when paperwork is mentioned. How do you store it so that it can be easily accessed? Before addressing this issue, I'd like to make an analogy. We build an entire kitchen for the purpose of preparing food, allocate a great deal of space for it, and spend large amounts of money on it. There are very few people, however, who have a similar attitude to household administration, even though this task is just as constant as cooking. Items for administrative work are often kept in various places and then spread out sporadically on the kitchen table. A bill gets put back on to a pile, only to disappear again into a drawer. Does this sound like you? As I see it, an area designated for office work is not a useless indulgence. Such an area offers a daily and weekly solution to getting it all done, because it's the home base for all the paper that enters through your mailbox.

A desk and appropriate chair are essential for a smooth-running administrative system. This system should be within arm's reach, for retrieving all categories of personal and business papers. First and foremost, make your system practical. The following is a description of how I've organized my administrative system at home. I'm not suggesting that you imitate my methods; I just aim to inspire new ideas.

✔ TIP

Make your office attractive as well as practical, so that being there feels good.

Imagine a built-in-cupboard filled mostly with books, and an extended pull-out desk.

✓ TIP

_____

Keep the paperwork you use most often in an accessible place. Sit down. The things you can reach from a sitting position are what I consider accessible. This is the most important spot in your office area, similar to the top drawer in your kitchen.

Is your administrative work draining? Tackle it at the time of day you're at your best. If you're a morning person, schedule an hour one morning and sit down to do the job.

My best tip for administrative work: Sit down and do it. It sounds simple and it is. It's calming; it encourages precision in your organization and helps to complete the job at hand. In other words, give yourself the time you need.

A logical division is the first thing to keep in mind. The second is system maintenance. In my case this is one evening a week. For a while, this was always a Friday evening, though the days vary at the moment. On my selected evening I sit down to work; sitting down is crucial.

My watch hangs there on a nail when I'm at home. There is also a photo and a small box with some pens and pencils, as well as my appointment diary. There's a shelf under the desk where I keep my "chore pile." On the shelf above my head are paperclips, drawing pins, scissors, glue, tippex and ink. On a shelf above that are greeting cards, stationery, stamps, addresses and envelopes. The telephone is on my right and to my left I have a small cupboard on wheels with three drawers. If you had an aerial view of these drawers, you would see my entire administration. One drawer contains registration papers, ID cards, membership cards, medical cards, vouchers, business cards and sunglasses. The middle

---

✓ TIP

If you've decided which things you want to accompany you through life, you can look into a suitable "saving system," or a new way to display a collection. If you decide to have a new cupboard built, take the time to choose something you won't get tired of. If you want something more informal, a do-it-yourself system is handy. As the years go by or with a change in needs, shelves can be added or rearranged.

I settle all practical and financial business to the best of my ability. If it's necessary, you can assign yourself more than one day a week. It works for me, and my business is sufficiently in hand.

---

drawer contains bank statements. The bottom drawer is filled with hanging-folders. I've created a system for the different categories that I use most frequently. In a moment I'll describe a method you can adopt for your own use.

If I look at my pile of things to do, I see:

A postcard with insufficient postage

A dental bill for my insurance company

An invoice for a book I've ordered

Information about a course, which I've not yet decided whether or not to take

A folder with my preparations for a lecture

A key I need to return; I also want to add a note

A birth announcement from a friend who just had a daughter. I plan to send a gift.

This is the sum of the past week. I will attend to it on Thursday evening and I've made a note in my pocket diary. Imagine there's glue on your fingers. Take one of your own papers and

✍ **Exercise 10**

Sit down with your paperwork for an hour. Look at the time when you start. If necessary set a timer and keep working until it goes off. What do you need to keep you doing the job? A pen, pencil, Post-it notes, staples, a wastepaper basket, folders for bank statements, a telephone … make your own additions. If you don't have what you need, be sure to get it.

This hour is for working, and taking care of the mail is work. Do a thorough job. Put away what needs to be saved immediately. The rest can go with the wastepaper to be recycled. Is there any paperwork left over? Does it need its own folder? Give this folder a temporary name. You can resume the task during the next administrative hour.

Assign yourself a "mail-tackling hour" once a week for the next six weeks. Note this in your diary or on a calendar. Use this hour for going through the mail and refining your retrieval system.

Reaction

This is from a musician following a combined effort to organize her sheet music: "All the music I need can now be located in four different folders: Études and lesson material, recital pieces, concerts and sonatas. Moreover, I have everything in a computer file that can be sorted according to the level of difficulty. My student file is automated and all assignments are saved on an old computer near the piano. Notebooks have become redundant. My students get a printout of their lessons and I have an insight into what each one is doing.

"In the beginning, it looked like a few of the students who knew me well would faint on the spot, when they realized I could find their assignments within ten seconds."

✔ TIP

Label your new system right away. It takes some getting used to.

make a decision about it. Make a phone call or send a note, but do something about it! I only remove the glue after the action is completed and not a moment earlier. The papers I'm finished with are put on the pile for recycling or in the appropriate hanging-folders in the cupboard on wheels. When I'm done with the pile, one pile still remains, which holds all the chores which require more information before they can be completed — I want to send photos to a friend, but I still need his change of address; a claim for travelling expenses still awaits a reaction; I've signed up for a business forum, but have yet to receive the definite programme. I go quickly through these things and am reminded of all the loose ends still needing to be finalized.

I've set up paperwork files for a number of clients containing the documents and papers frequently needed. If you

✔ TIP

Administration requires a retrieval system, not a saving system. While putting things away ask yourself: Where do I want to find it and what will make sense a year from now? You can find papers by putting them in a hanging folder system according to subject, a box folder, or a ring binder with dividers.

want to do this yourself you'll need loose folders, labels, an empty table and two hours of your time. These are the necessary ingredients for creating a general, as well as a temporary, classification.

Sort your piles according to subject matter. I have a separate folder for telephone papers, train travel, my bike, subscriptions, instruction folders, sales slips, city information, and the like. If you sort everything first the different categories will automatically become apparent. Make sub-categories from the biggest heaps. For example, sort the piles with insurance papers according to insurance type. File them away consistently and label them clearly. Is a file for matters pertaining to your home a good idea? What about your child's nursery care, diplomas, gas, light and water? And then there's the one for recommended restaurants and cafes. The contents of this file are a source of ideas, as are the four folders over directions in which you may travel. I've labelled these North, South, East and West. If I plan a visit north I refer to the articles I've cut out about that region.

> ✓ TIP
>
> One student is happy about her system for photographs. She puts them away immediately in an album with transparent pockets. She has an album for each of her children. She dates the negatives and stores them in a shoebox.

Your personal categories will be spread out on the table after an hour and a half of sorting. This you can count on, if you can only resist the temptation of reading the material. If a new task comes along set it aside for another moment. Finish categorizing first!

You can give your newly made folders a temporary label — a coloured Post-it note, for example. Arrange the folders according to subject: financial business, insurance, deeds and contracts, and put them in the cupboard or cabinet in alphabetical order. The time invested initially will be a time saver in the long run. That's something to look forward to. Moreover, sorting is a calming activity. As a child I would play "office." My girlfriends and I would find an old pair of reading glasses amongst my parents' things and put our hair in buns. Then we would make important calls and use the typewriter while speaking correctly and distinctly.

Food for thought

A discussion about unsolicited mail came up during one of my lessons. "I never read it," said one. "I want to stay informed," said another. A third commented, "I only go through it if I'm looking for something specific." What should you do with all this printed matter?

One person in the group cut out interesting offers and put them in a kitchen drawer. She cleaned out the drawer when it was full.

Learning by playing ... But back to the here and now ...

If a piece fits in more than one category, you can make a copy or put a reference note in the other folder. For instance, you can arrange the folders' contents according to their arrival date.

Take a look in an office equipment store, if you prefer something other than a cupboard with hanging-folders; you'll find framed hanging-file folders consisting of twenty-five folders; expansion folders with multiple pockets; ring binders with file pockets and dividers. Shoeboxes can be handy if you construct partitions and label them. One participant in a course I gave one autumn attained some fame with a small crate dubbed, "Jo's crate." This crate had been transformed into a reminder system, many years before. She had made twelve partitions in it, each marked with a month of the year. In it she arranged papers she didn't need until a certain month. For example, she put a February dinner invitation, accompanied by directions, in the back of the February section. A greetings card from an acquaintance whom she definitely wanted to send a Christmas card was put in the December section. Thus she kept track of upcoming business.

Secretaries have different systems for staying informed of

forthcoming appointments which can also be applied at home. Everyone also has his or her own creative ideas. I have come across alphabetic systems for recipes or children's songs. Everything that you want to be easily accessible can be organized, whether by a paper system or electronically.

If you've come to the point where you can determine the main categories after two hours of sorting, then you've made a good start; put your work aside and do something else. Continue with the contents of the main folders during your weekly administration evening, after you've taken care of more pressing matters. Thus you bring a semblance of order to your mass of paperwork. What a wonderful feeling! No

---

✍ Exercise 11

This exercise demonstrates the results of a clean-up task. It's easy to forget how things used to be. With photos taken before and after a clean-up you can compare two different given moments. The actual work that has taken place in-between is invisible. This is the best possible way to observe Hestia.

Take a picture of your business administration area in its present state. Arrange your piles of folders — and other papers — for photographing. Paste or tape the picture on the left-hand-side of an open notebook and note the date.

Take a picture of your business administration area after you've completed the clean-up and reorganization of your papers. Tape this picture to the opposite page and note the date.

You might also choose something besides your administrative work to photograph; clothing, shoes, a pantry or a bookcase are all good subjects for recording an image of "before and after." Your progress becomes visible and this is something to be proud of.

more time wasted on searching through heaps of paper, and more energy for the good life.

An acquaintance of mine is an Egyptologist; a university lecturer who also gives lectures to the general public on her area of expertise. She also runs courses on ancient Egyptian culture and gives guided tours. She possesses around ten thousand slides, and shows some to her audience during lectures. "Temples Dedicated to Gods" is one such category. Others are: "Grave Relics," "Coptic Art" and "Museum Reliefs." Within each category she has made a chronological division between the oldest and most recent dynasties

True Story

A woman called me at my office, wanting assistance with her administration so we made an appointment. Her house appeared spacious and was tastefully decorated. She had a mirror with a gilded frame and a comfy couch to dream away in. She opened a cupboard door and indicated two piles. "Well, there it is," she said with a meek look. To get to the crux, we placed the whole batch on the table, and it appeared that the majority of the envelopes were still unopened. She was so afraid of confronting bad financial news — that did not exist! — that she didn't dare to look. The result of our work was sorted bank papers, correspondence with her lawyer, medical bills and bills for odd jobs. We also settled some phone calls. She already had a suitable box for hanging folders.

Six months later she called back and we dealt with the mail once again. This way she was able to get back on track once more. To keep up, she now takes part in a bi-weekly group where the participants encourage each other and aid one another with concrete assistance. I feel she did a good job in getting over the hurdle, first with professional help and then with help and feedback from a support group.

and those in-between, for future use. This serves as a good retrieval system. Moreover, she keeps the slides in transparent folders, so with the use of a light frame she can easily verify which slides are in which folders' pockets.

 Tip

Keeping loose items in baskets helps to create order in a cupboard. Baskets holding socks or underwear are common examples. All it takes is one simple reach, and you've got what you need.

Aside from this, she's made various lists pertaining to different themes. If she wants to gather information about Isis and Osiris for an upcoming expedition, she refers to the list where she's made note of where to find the folders containing the relevant slides. If she's asked to lecture on Horus' eye, then she searches her collection and sets out to make a new list on the subject. Due to her vast knowledge, she has a wealth of information in her memory. This seems to be a tremendous help in dealing with a complicated system. But if she were to stop working in this area regularly, her system would no longer function optimally.

A friend of hers has a photography collection on the same subject, though her approach is different. She arranges her collection according to temples and museums. This is possible because she has a photographic memory of the location of objects. Are you looking for that blue vase with the image of the gazelle head? It's in the museum in Stockholm. She's able to locate the photograph with the sought-after vase in no time.

Contradiction in terms

And now to the business at hand ... what was the business anyway?

In both of these cases retrieval is made possible by a self-created classification in combination with memory. Likewise, the arrangement of your own things at home always has to do with their function. This is subjective and personal. Through usage you discover what works best for you. You can make adjustments to your system now and then. A database can be installed on your computer, where you designate each item with identifying marks for finding later.

Do you know anyone who has ever experienced a house fire? They can tell you which papers are best stored in a fireproof vault, whether at the bank or at home. Keep the

---

The spoon (3)

The following is the continuing story of the stolen spoon: I called my friend Bas to ask him if he knew what had happened to the spoon I had given him. I confessed that I had stolen it and then given it to him to be rid of it. He only seemed to really understand the implication at the end of our conversation. A few days later I received an envelope from him in the mail, and yes, it contained "the spoon." He told me that he'd stirred his coffee with it for many years while watching the evening news. It landed in a container with pens when he moved house, and was no longer in use.

And fifteen years later there it was, right in front of me. It had resurfaced. It seemed like the right moment to give this item a more appropriate place in my life. Bas still considered it to be his. I agreed and he got it back once more.

I'm presently trying to find the store it came from. I can't remember the name but I do know where it was located. I'll have to travel to get there. What can I possibly say when I get there? You'll be hearing from me.

original papers in the safe and make copies for your filing system. I know a woman who keeps many copies for a friend. Her friend in turn, does the same for her. This is a safety measure. An insurance agent can offer detailed advice.

~ 7 ~

Making a Clean-up Plan

Looking ahead and liking it

In chapters three, four and five, you've become acquainted with the behaviour of objects that exist under the same roof as you. It's therefore helpful to understand how to *shape* this co-existence. Are you in charge of your things, or is it *their* house that you live in? Does living around them give you a feeling of freedom or restriction? Can you move forward or are they obstructing your path?

What's the point of making plans to clean up your entire house?

I hear from my clients and students that the motivating factors come from their environment as well as from within. Here are some examples:

You are going to move house in six months and want to clean up, to avoid packing a lot of things which you won't have use for.

The cupboards and desktops in your spare room are jam-packed and things are overflowing on to the floor. You want to do something about it.

Neither you nor your partner throws things away. The house is getting cramped with all the cupboards and boxes, and it's getting annoying.

You've begun to notice that you're relocating piles of items.

If you want to clean up, you don't have a clue where to put them, and they just land on another heap. Looking for things is getting on your nerves.

You've stored items from your late parents in boxes; you want to go through them in your own good time.

You've had health problems for years and a backlog is the result. You'd like to tackle it, but are only able to work for short periods and don't want to neglect the daily household chores.

You're moving to smaller quarters. (Whoops! That's one for advanced students.)

You want to reorganize the belonging of those no longer living with you (ex-partners, grown children) and store them in one place, instead of having them scattered through the house.

There are nooks and crannies that haven't been tidied up in years, because there's so much clutter. You feel it's time for a change.

You've taken a good look at your past with a therapist's help. This has motivated you to give your house a thorough clean. Where should you start?

The old kitchen cupboard needs relocating because the kitchen is being redesigned. Moving it upstairs will mean re-organizing up there, because the office equipment will probably have to be moved to the attic. The kitchen has triggered a chain reaction.

If nothing is bothering you, your family members or your housemates, then there's no need for a clean-up. Continue living life to the fullest. Periodic maintenance and a thorough clean of all the cupboards and corners now and then will suffice. It's a liberating feeling to live in a house where the entire backlog has been eliminated.

However, certain places are bound to be neglected and will need a good clean out as the months and years pass. I have my knitting needles in a cylindrical case in an out-of-the way corner, stored with a rug beater, a broom, an old coat rack and some wooden slats. Now, about nine years later, I've started to knit a cap and I've cleaned out the corner. Most of the items have been relocated. This is an illustration of the natural course that our things take — namely, use, standing still (out of sight, out of mind) and revival. Following a camping trip your tents and camping equipment can be inspected, repaired, cleaned and put away as I did with the items in the corner. This approach allows these places to continue to take part in the household rhythm, even though it may be a slow one. Whether quick or slow, rhythms are an essential part of what was described in Chapter Two.

You should however realize that backlogs are quite different. They consist of chores that no longer keep up with the rhythm of the household, or are no longer able to reach its *temperature*. This chapter deals with eliminating backlogs. How do you go about it while keeping up with your daily responsibilities?

Extra work involves more time. This is the case in every enterprise, as it is in the business of your household. It's a project. The following is a real life example:

Three years ago a woman who lived on her own was feeling fatigued and inert. The clutter in her home was discouraging. During our home appointment we took a good look at her daily and weekly schedule, and established a daily clean-up hour for her administrative work, starting with her tax statements. She gave up a language course she hardly ever attended due to her lack of stamina, and the plan was to have the paperwork organized by the second visit.

During our coffee break her favourite hobby came up; she spent much of her time painting and loved it. She took a painting course and worked in a studio. The problem was that she felt she wasn't spending enough time painting at home. The table needed to be moved into the sunlight, but the large cupboard next to it was an obstacle. Where could the cupboard go? There would have been an alternative spot in the living room, if she didn't have to sleep there on a make-shift bed. There were so many boxes and bags in her bedroom that it couldn't be used for its actual purpose. She wanted to go through those boxes at some point and take some of the contents to the attic. That horrible attic — first finding the key was a problem, then it was two flights up, there was a missing lightbulb, a broken window and two locks to prevent robbery. No, she did not enjoy being in the attic!

Slowly but surely her story hit home. And I bet it sounds familiar. She's surely not the only one with a backlog at home. After conferring, we decided on a new approach. We designed a step-by-step plan, which meant: first, sorting out the attic, and then getting the bedroom in order for its original purpose. Afterwards the extra bed could be removed from the living room, and the cupboard could be placed in another corner. Finally the table could be pushed to the spot in the sunlight.

It's my pleasure to report our success; step-by-step we achieved all that we set out to do. The attic was organized, the administration sorted out, the bedroom restored, and the extra bed was put away in the attic. The table found its place in front of the window with an easel and several wall shelves for art supplies next to it. She also acquired a cupboard on wheels for her paints and brushes. We worked together nine mornings, once a month. In the meantime, she's been through boxes and bags, labelled and taken things away and had others removed. I also recall her having had an appointment with an insurance agent to review her policies and make necessary revisions.

Speaking of extra time and energy, my client devoted plenty of both to the task which was fantastic, but exhaustion and feelings of depression don't just dissolve into thin air. She had to struggle through. She realized that letting go of her possessions was not her greatest strength, and she still has the tendency to hold on to them. Still, something significant took place. She applied to art school and was accepted, and she now makes the most of her studio space.

TIP

If you discover forgotten chores while cleaning up — a large pile of ironing, for example — it might be wise to have someone else do the job, just this once. This also applies to repair jobs. Make a note of these and take care of them later. You could also hire someone to do them for you, as a one-off. Finish the corner or room you are working on before moving on to forgotten chores.

Doing this work made her more flexible in disposing of half-read newspapers, piles of magazines, unworn clothing and whatever forms a stumbling block. We wrote a report on our collaborative clean-up project together at its conclusion.

I'm sure you understand that nine months of cleaning do not guarantee a perfect life. It does however provide a breathing space for the future. The above plan came to fruition because this woman was able to express what she "truly" wanted. We always want so much, but what are our real inner longings? The "heart's desire" phenomenon, in the above illustration, showed the way to a step-by-step plan, and we can assume that this is why it

TIP

Completing a job provides energy. Finish a job completely. Loose ends count. You will feel the burden lift.

✔ TIP

Allow yourself enough rest during a clean-up chore. Allocate yourself some free time every day of every week, and keep this time free. Don't cheat by making chore-related arrangements. Allowing free time takes some effort but rewards you with some space in your life. Imagine what you can do with it!

worked so well. A plan conceived at the drawing board is often just theory. A plan that springs from inner longing contains a goal, and therefore has real meaning. While we were puffing and panting in the attic, we knew that we were working towards a place to paint. This helps to get the job done. There's great power in true longing, which we used to our advantage.

Now it's your turn. Ask yourself what you really want. You could end up with a long list if you make note of it all. You can voice your wishes out loud in your room, or write them down on a large sheet of paper. As long as they are expressed, you open the way to communicating your inner wishes to yourself.

Doctors experience something similar during visiting hours. A patient may enter with a variety of questions and complaints. An examination follows and then comes advice or a prescription. Just as the patient is leaving he or she may turn and say, "Oh yes, one more thing, Doctor ..." That which is most essential is hidden deep inside you. It's the place we sometimes land while dreaming, reading or taking a stroll. All it takes is a moment when you've escaped from the normal pace of daily living.

The following assignment was done with the participants on one of my first household courses. Make a note of what makes you feel warm (we were discussing fire and heat). Everyone is enthusiastic about, or is inspired, by something.

Finding satisfaction with your achievements is an art. Receiving joy from labour sounds like a throwback to the nineteenth century. Those involuntarily unemployed, however, realize the significance of work. The Swedish author, Astrid Lindgren, portrays a house elf in her *Tomten* books. Many writers describe the importance of household work, and the theme of their books — experiencing pleasure from daily labour — helps you to see your own work from a fresh angle.

Then there are circumstances that make us burn with rage or blow up in frustration. Instead of taking a psychological approach we spoke of real-life experiences. One person feels passionate about child rearing; another about organizing a collection of food packages, blankets and toys for children in a refugee camp in the Balkans. This passion can be expressed either within or outside the home in activities such as carrying out chores with the aim of de-cluttering: creating a good recipe file for a cooking hobby; preparing a room to start working from home; making a special table in the corner of a room; or keeping an orderly administration for the organization of freight transport. These are all examples that take place within the home.

Do you have comparable wishes and chores on your list? Are they taunting you by telling you that you'll never follow through? Just assume that you will and you'll be the one who laughs last. Let's now move on to a step-by-step plan.

If it's not heart's desire that is motivating you, but simply the will to clean up, then the approach is somewhat different. Make use of the chore list in Exercise 7 on page 66, and leave two empty columns at the top. Take it with you as you move through your house. Ask yourself in each room or area how you imagine it in the future. What is your aim regarding the

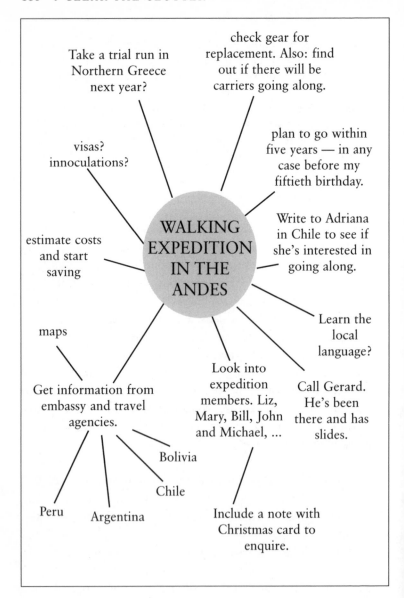

Take a trial run in Northern Greece next year?

check gear for replacement. Also: find out if there will be carriers going along.

visas? innoculations?

plan to go within five years — in any case before my fiftieth birthday.

WALKING EXPEDITION IN THE ANDES

Write to Adriana in Chile to see if she's interested in going along.

estimate costs and start saving

Learn the local language?

maps

Look into expedition members. Liz, Mary, Bill, John and Michael, ...

Call Gerard. He's been there and has slides.

Get information from embassy and travel agencies.

Bolivia

Chile

Peru   Argentina

Include a note with Christmas card to enquire.

Step 1

If there's something you long for, make a mind map, as described in Exercise 8 (page 74). Instead of writing "my life," in the middle, note down your heart's desire. Draw or write anything that's required to ensure you achieve it, around these words. You'll find an example on the opposite page. My example is a desire to take a hiking tour through the Andes Mountains. If you want to realize a dream, you can create space for this in your home. Set up certain areas for doing this and spend time there preparing. Clean-up chores might be necessary to create a suitable place. List these and leave room for two empty columns.

If you have a heart's desire and you have a list of chores needed to reach your goal, it might be fun to make a colourful collage. This can be done with drawings, magazine cuttings and photographs glued on to a large sheet of paper. I saw one once on a client's kitchen door and it works as an incentive to have a project hanging in clear view. In business this is referred to as a project plan. This version is even better.

Step 2

Organize your list according to chore type:
  Do-it-yourself
  Ask for advice or quote from …
  First discuss with parties concerned
  Do it with …
  Get rid of … etc.
  These things go in the first empty column.

space where you're now standing? Most likely a number of clean-up and decorating chores need to be done to achieve your goals. You put these on the list. Be prepared, the list may become rather long. Don't be discouraged; it's just a list. Sleep on it for a night or two.

It doesn't matter if your chore list has been motivated by sunlight in a room or a tour through your house. What does matter, is that you have it ready. I'm obviously not in the right position to judge it from here. Maybe the sequence for tackling your chores is obvious from the start, and then again, you might be at a total loss. If the latter applies, an in-between step is called for.

In some cases I ask the client to write down each chore on an individual card instead of working with a list. This results in a box full of cards. Cards are handy because you can

---

Step 3

Put the chores in the right sequence. Ask yourself: What has to happen before I can start with this or that job?

If cleaning the hall depends on making space in the shed, you should understand that the shed comes first. The hall can then be done in no time.

If new chores come up while you are working on the shed, add them to the list, but finish the hall first. This is especially important when it comes to time-consuming work, such as sanding and varnishing a cupboard. This type of work can really slow down the plan's progress.

New things, once on the list, can be included in the project as a whole. This gives a clearer view of the total situation and minimizes the chance that you'll get discouraged and give up.

Use the second empty column to give your chores a number that corresponds with their planned sequence, or with the amount of time you think they'll take.

spread them out on the table as if in a game. You can look at them with someone else and shuffle them. This was the method I used with a part-time working mother. We created piles as we shuffled; one was for her husband to attend to, one for outside contractors, another for chores still to be considered, and the last one was for chores to be started on right away. Completed chores were checked off. My client chose to save the cards. Another option is to tear them up and watch how your pile shrinks.

Step 4

Decide on the month that you think you'll be doing a specific chore. Check your diary or calendar to see if this is feasible and note it down in pencil. This way you remind yourself of your decision, but can still make changes if necessary.

Some jobs may be connected to circumstances or weather. Think about indoor jobs in the autumn and winter; a job involving certain elements, because your sister is coming to visit from Australia; or cleaning up the garage before your partner's birthday because he or she is getting a new bike.

By determining the month for a particular job, you create an immediate overview of what's involved. For the time being, you can forget about the jobs to be tackled six months from now. That allows the peace of mind and focus you need to do the job at hand. Keep holidays and vacation times in mind. These call for extra planning and time. Don't plan too much around these periods.

Evaluate the plan regularly to check if it is moving along as intended. Make modifications as you see fit. A captain is aware of the course his ship sails during a voyage, and adjusts it in order to reach his destination.

✓ TIP

Endurance is usually more likely with time-oriented chores than with result-oriented chores. Decide beforehand how long you want to spend on your clean-up chore and stop on time. Be content with the results. You've got other things to do and tomorrow is a brand new day. If you work to get results and you definitely want that cupboard finished, you put yourself under pressure. You might even get it done, but it takes away from the pleasure of accomplishing the task. The end result is mounting resistance felt the next day. Spare yourself and take as much time as you need for a chore. You'll only know for sure how much time is involved after the task is completed.

The moment has arrived for some last minute decisions before the final kick-off.

Have you allotted an entire day or week for your clean-up plan? Will you be asking for help and, if so, who will you ask? Are you allowing yourself an hour per job because you'll have to fit the jobs in between your daily tasks? Have you established your working sequence and would you like to have feedback from someone? These are facets of managing. The project in your enterprise is about to begin. You're dealing with the final preparations.

When the day comes for your first job, determine beforehand what time you'll stop. This is the only unconditional requirement. If you need a reminder, you can set your alarm fifteen minutes before the designated time. You should realize that it's hard to estimate the time a job will take. Rearranging a cupboard takes two afternoons, not one and a half hours. Some people multiply their estimate by two or three. Analysing a finished job helps you to gain insight and enables you to estimate accurately.

There was one thing my girlfriend, Ulrike, wanted to accomplish before moving abroad. She had always hoped to one day give her three sons photo albums of their youth; she wanted to have the photos organized before the move. We prepared a long table, on loan from her neighbour, in her guest room. On it were transparent insert folders, adhesive labels and piles of photographs. She sorted them by year, while I put them in temporary folders and wrote the year on adhesive labels. She spent many an evening on the chore. The photos have since been sorted out and accompanied her when she moved. The job of putting them in their albums lies in the future.

When the time comes to start with your initial chore — the shed, for example — the first thing to do is to put items together according to category. Give the garden equipment one corner. The same goes for tools and bike gear; toys can go in a crate. This gives you the overview you need. Now you can sort through by group and decide what can go. With this in mind, create a departure area, by placing a box or crate near the door. Designate another box for items to be taken back to the house. Try not to be tempted to walk back and forth from the shed to the house. The things meant for inside will reach their destination in due course, when you have to go back to the house anyway. The shed is where you have to be now.

Organize the shed practically and logically. Frequently used tools should be easily accessible; decide what to do with

Two ex-students now visit each other every six months following a clean-up course. They check each other's progress and give feedback. They take their work seriously and behave like colleagues. I was pleasantly surprised when I heard about it.

> **✓ TIP**
>
> If you need a bit of support, tell someone about your plan. You might want to ask for advice, blow off some steam, or even complain about the work. Having people to support you helps you to go on. Don't be too proud to ask, it can be an inspiration for all involved.

those broken and hardly used items. Chores discovered along the way should be placed on the big list for the time being. Finally, after completing the job, you can clean and spruce up the shed. I've washed the windows in a corner after tidying up with a client. You'll notice how the extra touch influences a space. It's as if it feels friendlier and charged with energy. This energy helps you to maintain the space, and makes it a pleasant place to be.

> Student: "It's not more things we want, it's more room."

Stop working on time. The chores have been waiting so long that another week won't make much difference. There are other things that need your attention today. Don't go overboard by staying up until three in the morning because you feel compelled to get the bookcase finished.

If you're only able to work for an hour on a certain project, than pick a job you think you can do within that hour. Were you aware that eighty percent of all jobs can be done according to this "hour method?" Experience teaches that eighty percent of the work is done in twenty percent of the time allotted. The other twenty percent takes eighty percent of the time. If you keep this in mind, you won't be discouraged following a flying start.

When you start with a clean-up project, you should understand that it's like the tide; each plan has its own cycle of ups

> ✔ TIP
>
> Are you behind with putting your photos in albums? Start with this year's and keep it up. Take care of photos from years past when you have some extra time.

and downs. There will be moments of flowing with the current and then it will be still again. However, new opportunities arise. If this is clear, you'll do fine. During an ebbing tide the pace is slower; when the tide is rising the tempo increases again. That's simply the way it goes. Move with the current and don't try to force yourself into an inflexible plan. Forget about rigid planning before you even start.

You have to be loyal to persevere with the project. Stay motivated by keeping it varied and taking enough breaks. Although major jobs go on your list; try to do the minor ones as you encounter them along the way. Do you have any idea how long your project will take? This could vary from a few months to a few years, though as long as you are aware of the high and low aspects, you'll even be able to endure five years, if that's what it takes.

A year later, how's the situation looking? When I meet ex-students and clients, I naturally ask

> ✔ TIP
>
> Realize, as you plow through your things that the life stories connected to them surface simultaneously. Something occurs on two levels. The effect is positive, because how you relate to those story-filled objects changes through the years, because you too have changed. It becomes apparent the moment you clean up. It might be easy to deal with, but it could also be harder than expected. In the latter case, put the chore on hold for the time being and continue with the main job. It's enough to take care of one thing at a time.

them how everything has worked out. The ones who've forgotten how cluttered it used to be and have found workable solutions respond with a vague look. Others realize every day how much comfort their clean-up efforts have brought them. Then there are those who look back in disappointment; their attempts fell short of expectations during a vacation and came to a standstill.

During my course, "Running or Planning," I met three participants from an earlier programme. One had emptied out his entire storage shed; he had considered each and every item before having all of them removed for outside destinations. Another meticulously sorted through all her objects and clothing and decided what to save or discard; afterwards, she and her husband bought new cupboards, and she was thoroughly enjoying the brand new tidiness at home. The third had benefited most from the tips regarding habit forming, and the ironing and mending were going especially well.

Quote from a student on completion of a course: "I've gained the courage to persevere until I'm capable of loving my house again."

The last thing I want to share about a clean-up plan is this — a flexible approach works best. Work with a spirit free of clutter, as you unclutter your home. Allow yourself breathing space. Being too harsh on yourself is bound to lead to frustration. Isn't it your aim to create more breathing space at home? If you don't have a good feeling about your plan, don't hesitate to do away with it. Start with the chore which appeals to you most. A good start to a clean-up project is absolutely worth the effort.

✔ TIP

Realize that you can make plans for a certain day or even for a total period. You can't however always control outside forces. Work calmly and with commitment. Bend like a reed in the wind and spring back again. These words have a Zen ring to them, but I see it more as a dance or a conversation between you and life itself. You interact with one another and protect your own course of movement.

$\sim 8 \sim$

Remaining Odds and Ends

We'll always be left with certain places containing odds and ends. Is this something to worry about? Life is more dynamic than hanging folders and boxes. There's not always an ideal place for everything. A spectator on Earth is able to observe how the planet Venus depicts the shape of a large pentagon in the firmament. I've seen drawings of this phenomenon. Marking the exact spot where Venus appears in the zodiac results in these drawings. Over the course of weeks and months, the form of the path, which the planet has taken, materializes on paper. This is seen from an earthly perspective. This pentagon is, however, not totally complete. At the end of its journey the planet's position is slightly out of alignment with respect to the beginning. The figure therefore has a slight gap. A small piece is open — a leftover space of sorts.

This is also the case with objects, meals and this book, and so here I am, left with some scraps.

It's good policy to tackle a clean-up job and organize things categorically. Go right ahead. It will make it easier to have peace of mind. However, leftover objects will always remain. It's only by chance that you come across the slides from a trip taken long ago, or your old prizes.

This is the place for my loose ends. They might come in handy; who knows? They're worth as much as the rest, though this may seem slightly at odds with the message in the first seven chapters.

Order and Chaos

I spoke with my colleague, Yvonne, who also gives household organization courses, about order and chaos. She approached me after a lecture and brought up the subject of chaos. Is a cluttered shed necessarily in a state of chaos, or is it just a temporary backlog that could be made orderly in a flash? Maybe its owner just needs a pleasant spring day to bring the shed's contents outdoors, and hold a garage sale following a relaxing break. The principle of chaos is common to many stories of creation. Chaos is often the starting point and apparently a good beginning for an act of creation. It's a state of freedom and the possibilities are limitless. You can channel your longings and ideas in rearranging and recreating. In essence, you can make something from chaos, which reflects what is genuinely you, for now or the future.

Empty a cupboard completely. Surround yourself with the contents by placing them on tables and the floor. Now, that's chaos! This is a conscious act and happens to be the best way to organize and arrange the cupboard anew, according to your own needs. Chaos is the necessary opening for tidying and organizing. That's the way old structures are toppled.

This interplay between chaos, stability, destruction and reorganization is dynamic by nature. You can recognize this in history, with its revolutions and evolutions, as well as in the cycles of plants, season after season. Life with our possessions has a similar pattern. You co-exist within everyday reality, until suddenly a change occurs and you no longer want them in your life. The presence of chaos can offer the opportunity of a lifetime. It's the chance to make a complete turn around and a fresh start. You can see this in spring-cleaning and other purification rituals. A thorough clean-up at home serves the same end.

Yvonne and I spoke of order and chaos, as I'm doing now in this last drawer filled with odds and ends.

A Clean-up Culture

Dinnertime is a stressful moment for tidying up at home. You're making last minute cooking preparations or are hurriedly setting the table. The children are expected to clean up and wash their hands. At five or six o'clock everyone is tired after a busy day, which is therefore not the best moment for tidying. Before you know it you've lost your temper and are shouting. Tidying up receives a nasty association; it's forced and something to avoid. To maintain a pleasant atmosphere it's advisable to choose other times for cleaning up.

Turn teaching clean-up skills into a project. Demonstrating and making children follow your example is the best method for very young children; regular cleaning up together works well for older children, and staying on top of things and maintaining your sense of humour is the way to approach teenagers. This calls for effort on your part — and then there's still your partner or spouse.

Read the following tips to see which ones may come in handy. Some have appeared in previous chapters:

— Let everyone at home know when you intend to spend extra time cleaning, or are planning a clean-up project.
— Agree to suitable spots for migrating objects like scissors and keys. Label the new places until everyone is accustomed to them.

A father of two teenagers, who was responsible for the washing, made it clear that he would only wash the laundry found in the laundry basket. The children were sometimes out of clean socks because their dirty ones were under the beds. The solution to the problem was in their hands. All they had to do was put the dirty laundry where it belonged. He was stimulating good clean-up habits by confronting them with the consequences of their actions.

The agreement as to "who's in charge of what," helps to maintain a low level of annoyance (see Chapter Six).

A woman with three small children made rounds through the kitchen and living room every evening before going to bed. She picked up all of her kids' and husband's roaming objects and put them in a basket under the stairs. If they were missing something, they could search through the basket. If they wanted to keep track of their things, cleaning up on time was the solution.

A house conference for clean-up matters should be held now and then with household members. What is understood with the term "tidy room?" Discuss how to keep a room in good order.

The infamous rota of table setting and dishwashing, so that everyone gets a turn, is a common method. Vacations and outside activities call for reassessment now and again.

The family chore hour is one of my personal favourites (see Chapter Two). Something is accomplished, the family works together, both activity and time-out are exercised and a house culture is encouraged. This buzzing activity can also be found in a nursery-school class; you can hear by the noise what the mood is inside, just as in the family chore hour.

Ownership is Losing Significance

I read in a newspaper an interview with the philosopher, Jeremy Rifkin. Based on his observations of wealth and economic growth, he concludes that ownership is losing its significance. He asserts that material possessions can no longer keep up with the fast pace of today's economy. If your computer will be obsolete in the near future due to an outdated operating system, than renting makes more sense than buying. Using without owning is the upcoming trend. Instead of buying actual goods we'll be paying for access to them. Rental contracts and subscriptions to services are what the

The spoon (4)

I still owe you the end of the spoon story. I went back to the town where the shop from which I took it fifteen years earlier, was located. The shop no longer exists. By asking in the neighbourhood stores, I was able to discover the name of the former owners, a couple, and the town they had moved to after selling the building and inventory. I called, and the woman answered the phone. I confessed my theft and as compensation, I suggested a copy of my book as soon as it was printed. She liked the idea and found the story intriguing. She had naturally been confronted with more notable shoplifting cases and shared these with me. By virtue of the entire story and as far as I'm concerned, the spoon was finally able to reach the right temperature. Thanks to the writing of this book, the incident has come to light.

future holds. Don't buy a garden sprinkler; hire a company to do the job. Rent a walking service for the dog and take your child to daycare. Lease a car, computer, central heating boiler and a carpet. It's someone else's responsibility and yours to make use of. Is this what we have to look forward to?

The circumstances regarding our possessions in another one hundred, or even one thousand, years depends partly on us. A love of life and caring for the whole mosaic of living are concepts shaped by the times we live in.

Considering our over-full homes located in densely-populated regions this theme is most relevant today. What can be learned from an overdose of objects? Clean up and find out.

Departure Hall

There are benches situated on either side of the hallway in homes in the coldest part of Russia. Shoes, boots and slippers — set slightly apart — can be found under the benches. On entering a home, you take off your coat and sit down on the bench to remove your shoes and put on slippers. You then go into the main room, where you meet each other and socialize with conversation, music or the like. At the end of your visit you thank your hosts for their hospitality, gather your belongings and put on your coat. The host accompanies you to the hall to see you off. You sit down on the bench together as you put your shoes on again. It's the "departure bench" where any final thoughts can still be spoken before the last goodbyes. After all subjects have been exhausted and all pleasantries have been exchanged, what's left is there to save and cherish.

As we reach the book's end, it's time for both reader and writer to put our shoes back on. As I step into mine, I'd love you to join me on the bench, while I fasten my laces, and tell me how you liked the book. I'd sincerely welcome hearing from you and have you share your clean-up experiences with me.

Inge van der Ploeg
Email: ploeg@wxs.nl

Bibliography

Eijgenstein, Y., *The Happy Worker*. Amsterdam 1998.

Kingston, K., *Clean Your Clutter With Feng Shui*. New York 1999.

Lindgren, A., *The Tomten*, Floris Books. Edinburgh 1995.

Rifkin, J., *The Age of Access: The New Culture of Hypercapitalism, Where all of Life is a Paid-For Experience*. J. P. Tarcher, 2001.

Steiner, R., *The Riddle of Humanity*, Steiner Press. London 1990.

St. James, E., *Simplify Your Life*. Hyperion, London 1997.